PSALMS EXPLAINED

PSALMS EXPLAINED

Understanding the Book and Its Message for Today

Samuel Whitaker

Part of the Bible for Modern Life Series

Ascent Press

Published by
Ascent Press

ISBN: 979-8-9997184-8-8

Printed in the United States of America

First Edition 2026

For those seeking clarity in the ancient words of Scripture.

CONTENTS

Disclaimer

This book provides an interpretive overview of the biblical text using historical scholarship and modern analysis tools. It is intended to help readers understand the themes, context, and message of the biblical narrative and is not intended to replace personal study of Scripture

Introduction

Why Psalms Still Matters

The book of Psalms is one of the most widely read portions of the Bible. For centuries, it has been used in prayer, worship, reflection, and moments of personal struggle. People return to its words during seasons of joy, grief, fear, gratitude, and hope. The Psalms speak to deeply human experiences, which is why readers across cultures and generations continue to find meaning in them.

Yet the Psalms are often approached in fragments. Many people know individual passages — Psalm 23, Psalm 51, Psalm 46, Psalm 121 — but fewer understand the book as a whole. The Psalms were not originally written as a random collection of spiritual poetry. They developed over time and were eventually arranged into a structured book that serves a broader purpose within the biblical narrative.

The poems emerged from real moments in Israel's history. They reflect political upheaval, national crises, personal failure, celebration, public worship, and the long search for justice and restoration. Some psalms express confidence and joy. Others wrestle openly with suffering and doubt. Together they form a record of how ancient communities and individuals responded to life's uncertainties while maintaining a relationship with God.

This diversity of expression is part of what makes the Psalms unique. Few other biblical books capture such a wide range of emotional experience. Instead of presenting faith as something detached from hardship, the Psalms acknowledge that belief often develops within tension, unanswered questions, and difficult circumstances. They articulate grief without dismissing hope. They express anger while still seeking justice. They celebrate joy without ignoring the reality of suffering.

For modern readers, however, the world behind the Psalms can feel distant. The cultural setting, historical references, and poetic structure are far removed from contemporary life. Without some orientation, the book may appear as a loose collection of spiritual reflections rather than a carefully shaped work. That impression, once formed, is difficult to shake — and it keeps readers from engaging with much of what the book actually offers.

This book aims to bridge that gap. Rather than examining every psalm individually, *Psalms Explained* focuses on the broader patterns within the collection: the historical circumstances that shaped its development, the recurring themes that run throughout the poetry, the structure that organizes its 150 poems into a unified whole, and the ways the Psalms continue to speak to enduring human questions.

The Psalms are not merely religious poetry preserved from the past. They are a record of how people wrestled with faith in the midst of real life — with uncertainty, injustice, gratitude, loss, and longing. Those experiences have not disappeared. The circumstances surrounding them have changed enormously, but the experiences themselves remain recognizable.

Understanding the Psalms more deeply changes how they are read. Passages that once seemed familiar begin to reveal their context. Psalms that once felt uncomfortable begin to make sense as honest voices from within a long tradition of faith. And the book as a whole begins to function the way it was always intended — not as a reservoir of isolated encouragements, but as a sustained conversation about what it means to live, believe, and keep seeking God in the middle of a world that does not always make those things easy.

That conversation is still open. The goal of this book is to help modern readers enter it.

Chapter 1

The Human Question

"How long, Lord? Will you forget me forever? How long will you hide your face from me? How long must I wrestle with my thoughts and day after day have sorrow in my heart?"
— Psalm 13:1–2 (NIV)

The Universal Language of Poetry and Song

Across cultures and throughout history, people have turned to poetry and song as ways of expressing experiences that ordinary language often struggles to contain. When joy becomes overwhelming, when grief cuts deeply into the heart, or when fear and uncertainty weigh heavily on the mind, individuals frequently reach for forms of expression that move beyond straightforward explanation. Music, poetry, and prayer allow people to give shape to emotions that might otherwise remain unspoken, offering a vocabulary for experiences that are difficult to capture in everyday conversation. These forms of expression do more than describe life; they help individuals process it. They allow the human heart to respond to moments of beauty, tragedy, longing, and hope in ways that resonate beyond simple words.

The book of Psalms belongs to this world of human expression. Rather than functioning primarily as a narrative or historical record, it preserves a collection of songs, prayers, and poetic reflections that emerged from the lived experiences of the people of ancient Israel. Within these writings are voices that celebrate moments of triumph and gratitude alongside voices that wrestle with sorrow, confusion, anger, and longing. The Psalms capture the full range of human emotion and demonstrate how faith interacts with the realities of everyday life. Instead of presenting belief as a purely intellectual exercise or a detached theological system, the Psalms reveal what faith looks like when it is lived out amid the uncertainties and challenges of real experience.

Readers often recognize this quality almost immediately when they encounter the Psalms. Unlike many other biblical books that focus on historical narratives or prophetic proclamations, the Psalms frequently speak in the first person. The words feel personal and immediate, as though the writer is speaking directly from the heart. These poems often sound like the reflections of someone wrestling honestly with life, someone who is willing to bring both confidence and confusion before God. Because of this tone, the Psalms often feel less like distant religious texts and more like conversations taking place in the present moment.

This deeply personal quality has helped the Psalms endure across centuries. People continue to return to these writings because they recognize something familiar within them. The questions, frustrations, and hopes expressed by the psalmists are not limited to a single culture or historical moment. They echo experiences that remain recognizable today. Whether someone encounters the Psalms during a season of joy or a time of grief, the words frequently resonate with the emotions they are experiencing. Understanding the Psalms begins with recognizing this reality: the book speaks to universal human concerns. Although the poetry emerged within the context of ancient Israel, the emotional and spiritual questions that shape the book remain relevant across generations.

The Search for Meaning

One of the most persistent questions people ask throughout history is simple yet profound: how should life be understood when circumstances become uncertain or painful? Human beings have wrestled with this question for thousands of years, attempting to make sense of suffering, injustice, and the unpredictable nature of existence.

Different cultures and traditions have approached this question in various ways. Philosophers have written extensively about the nature of happiness, justice, and the purpose of life. Religious traditions have developed systems of belief intended to explain the world and humanity's place within it. These approaches share a common instinct — the desire to arrive at an explanation that makes suffering comprehensible and hope reasonable.

The Psalms approach this question differently. Rather than presenting structured philosophical arguments or systematic theological explanations, they give voice to lived experience. The writers speak directly from the realities they face, describing moments of danger and betrayal alongside seasons of gratitude and awe. They do not step back from their circumstances to analyze them from a distance. They write from inside those circumstances, and that inside quality is what gives the Psalms their particular authority.

Some psalms celebrate moments of victory or deliverance, describing times when danger has passed and gratitude fills the heart. Others reflect seasons of distress and uncertainty, capturing moments when the writer feels surrounded by hardship. Still others express quiet trust even when circumstances remain difficult, demonstrating a confidence that does not depend entirely on external conditions having improved.

When these poems are read together, they create a portrait of faith that includes both confidence and struggle. This honesty is one of the most remarkable aspects of the Psalms. Many people assume that religious writings portray faith as something calm and settled, free from doubt or frustration. The Psalms challenge that assumption by revealing how belief often develops in the middle of confusion, disappointment, and unanswered questions. Rather than hiding those experiences, the psalmists bring them into the open and speak about them directly. The search for meaning, in the Psalms, is not something that happens before faith begins. It is something that happens within faith, continuously, as part of what it means to maintain a living relationship with God.

Speaking to God in Real Life

Another striking feature of the Psalms is the way the writers address God directly. Many of the poems are written as prayers spoken as though the writer expects God to hear and respond. This approach creates a tone of immediacy that feels deeply personal.

The psalmists do not simply speak about God from a distance; they speak to Him. They ask questions, express gratitude, confess failures, and plead for help. Sometimes their words carry a tone of calm reflection, while at other times they reveal urgency and emotional intensity.

For modern readers, this style can feel surprisingly candid. The Psalms contain expressions of frustration, grief, and even anger. Some writers ask why injustice appears to prevail, while others question why suffering continues despite their devotion. These questions are not presented as abstract theological debates. Instead, they appear as personal appeals spoken in moments of distress.

The presence of these questions reveals something important about the biblical understanding of prayer. Prayer in the Psalms is not limited to formal language or carefully structured statements. It includes honest conversation with God that reflects the full range of human experience. Doubt, confusion, longing, gratitude, and trust all appear within these prayers.

The Psalms suggest that faith does not require pretending that life is simple or free from difficulty. Instead, they encourage people to bring the full weight of their experiences into dialogue with God. This approach to prayer is one of the most practically significant features of the book. It widens the definition of what prayer can be. A person does not need to have arrived at peace before approaching God. The psalmists came with everything still unsettled, and their willingness to do so is part of what the book preserves and commends.

What makes this even more striking is how it differs from much of the religious writing that surrounded ancient Israel. Many prayers from neighboring cultures in the ancient Near East were formal and carefully prescribed — specific words offered to specific deities in specific ways, with little room for personal variation. The Psalms move in a different direction entirely. They present prayer as a form of genuine speech rather than recitation, as a living exchange rather than a ritual formula. The writers do not appear to be performing prayer according to a template. They are speaking from within their actual circumstances, bringing those circumstances before God in language that reflects what they are actually experiencing. That directness is unusual in the ancient world, and it is one of the reasons the Psalms stood out then and continue to stand out now.

The Emotional Range of the Psalms

Because the Psalms arise from real situations, they display a remarkable emotional range. Some psalms overflow with joy and gratitude, celebrating moments when life has taken a favorable turn. Others emerge from seasons of crisis, describing danger, illness, betrayal, or national hardship. Still others express a quiet confidence that persists even when circumstances remain uncertain — a trust that does not depend on external conditions having improved.

This emotional variety reflects the complexity of human life. Few people experience life as a single emotional state. Joy and sorrow often appear side by side, and confidence may exist alongside uncertainty. Rather than simplifying these realities, the Psalms acknowledge them. The writers move through moments of hope and despair, sometimes within the same poem. A psalm may begin with a description of distress and end with a declaration of trust, illustrating the internal movement of the writer's thoughts as they bring their experience before God.

Many psalms also follow a recognizable pattern of movement. A poem may begin with a plea for help, describing enemies or hardships that feel overwhelming. As it continues, the writer recalls earlier moments when God provided guidance or deliverance. These memories gradually reshape perspective, leading toward renewed confidence that the present difficulty will not define the final outcome. This movement does not necessarily mean that the external situation has changed. It reflects a shift within the writer — the kind of shift that can occur when experience is brought honestly into prayer rather than kept at a distance from it.

Individual Experience and Community Life

Although many psalms sound deeply personal, they were not written only for private reflection. The Psalms also played a significant role in the public worship of Israel. Ancient communities gathered to sing these songs during festivals, temple ceremonies, and national celebrations. Through repeated use, the words of the Psalms became part of the shared memory of the people.

A psalm may begin with the voice of an individual describing personal distress, yet as it unfolds, the language often expands to include the larger community. The writer's experience becomes a reminder that others share similar struggles. By expressing these emotions in a public setting, the Psalms helped individuals recognize that their experiences were not isolated. Joy, fear, gratitude, and grief were common elements of human life, and the

Psalms provided a framework through which communities could acknowledge those realities together.

This dual function — personal expression woven into communal worship — is part of what allowed the Psalms to persist across so many generations. They were not preserved merely as literary artifacts but as living texts that communities kept returning to because they continued to serve the same purposes: giving voice to individual experience and knitting that experience into a shared understanding of faith.

The Role of Memory

Another recurring feature of the Psalms is the importance of remembering. When facing hardship, many psalmists recall earlier moments when God intervened on behalf of the people. These memories serve as reminders that difficult circumstances are not the final chapter of the story. For ancient Israel, collective memory played a crucial role in shaping identity. Stories of deliverance, guidance, and restoration were repeated across generations, reinforcing the belief that God remained faithful to His people.

This practice of remembering does more than provide comfort. It reframes the present. When a writer recalls an earlier moment of deliverance, the current difficulty is placed within a larger narrative — one that has a history of resolution, even if resolution has not yet arrived. The present moment of hardship becomes one episode within a longer story rather than the whole story.

The most important memory that recurs throughout the Psalms is the story of the exodus — the account of God delivering Israel from slavery in Egypt and guiding the people through the wilderness toward a new land. This event functioned as the defining moment in Israel's national identity, the foundational evidence that God had acted on behalf of His people in real historical circumstances. When the psalmists faced new difficulties, they reached back to this story. They reminded themselves and their communities that the God they were addressing was the same God who had acted before, in ways that were concrete and verifiable within their own inherited history.

That grounding gave their prayers a different quality than appeals made into the unknown. They were calling on a God whose character had already been demonstrated, whose faithfulness had already been shown, and whose intervention was therefore not merely hoped for but argued for on the basis of what had already occurred. Several psalms make this appeal explicitly, recounting the events of the exodus in detail before turning to the present difficulty — as if to say: you have done this before, and what we are asking is consistent with who you have shown yourself to be.

For readers today, this same practice remains valuable even outside that specific historical framework. When individuals focus only on current circumstances, those circumstances can feel absolute. Memory introduces a longer view. It asks what else is also true, what has been navigated before, what earlier evidence might speak to the present difficulty. The psalmists practice this discipline consistently, and in doing so they model a way of thinking about life that prevents any single moment from bearing more weight than it should.

A Language for the Human Heart

Perhaps the most enduring contribution of the Psalms is the language they provide for experiences that are difficult to put into words. People often struggle to articulate their deepest emotions. Grief, gratitude, fear, and longing can all feel inadequate when expressed in ordinary speech. What is felt internally does not always translate easily into language.

The Psalms step into that gap. They offer vocabulary for experiences that resist simple description. Instead of forcing clarity too quickly, they allow space for honesty. A person can come with questions, frustration, or gratitude and find language that gives shape to those experiences. Some psalms move between distress and trust in ways that reflect how emotions actually shift rather than resolve all at once. They do not ask the reader to feel something different. They meet the reader where they are.

Part of what makes this possible is the way Hebrew poetry is constructed. Unlike much Western poetry, which relies heavily on rhyme and meter, Hebrew poetry works primarily through parallelism — the repetition and development of ideas across closely related lines. A statement is made, then restated in different language, or extended, or placed in contrast with its opposite. This structure reinforces meaning through repetition, allows a single thought to be approached from multiple angles, and creates a rhythm that is not dependent on a specific language — which is why the Psalms translate across cultures without losing their essential quality in the way that rhyming poetry often does.

The imagery the psalmists choose reinforces this effect. A shepherd guiding through difficult terrain, a fortress standing firm in a storm, a deer thirsting for water in a dry land — these images communicate not through definition but through recognition. Readers do not so much understand them as feel them. The shepherd image does not explain what care looks like; it evokes what care feels like. The thirst image does not describe spiritual longing analytically; it produces the sensation of it in the reader's own experience. That capacity to generate felt understanding rather than merely intellectual understanding is part of what gives the Psalms their lasting reach. They work on the reader at a level that prose argument typically cannot access.

This quality explains why the Psalms have been used so persistently across such different circumstances — at bedsides, in places of grief, in moments of unexpected joy, in the long quiet stretches of ordinary life. The poetry reaches experiences that prose often cannot, and it reaches them in a way that crosses the distance of centuries without losing its force.

Engaging with the Psalms today means entering a conversation that has been unfolding for thousands of years. Generations of readers have turned to these poems during moments of celebration, grief, uncertainty, and hope. Although the poems were written in a cultural setting very different from the modern world, they continue to speak to experiences that remain deeply familiar. The emotional and spiritual questions that shape the book have not disappeared with time. They are carried forward into each new era by people who recognize themselves in the same words.

In the chapters that follow, we will examine the historical setting in which these writings emerged, the structure that organizes the collection, and the themes that connect its diverse poems. Through this exploration, readers will gain a clearer understanding of how the Psalms function not only as individual expressions of faith but also as a carefully shaped book that reflects the enduring human search for meaning.

Chapter 2

Orientation

"Blessed is the one who does not walk in step with the wicked or stand in the way that sinners take or sit in the company of mockers, but whose delight is in the law of the Lord, and who meditates on his law day and night."
— Psalm 1:1–2

When readers first encounter the book of Psalms, it often feels noticeably different from many of the other books that appear in the Bible. Some biblical books unfold through narrative, tracing a sequence of events that gradually reveal a story about people, places, and historical developments. Genesis describes the origins of the world and the earliest generations of humanity, presenting stories about creation, family conflict, migration, and covenant. Exodus continues that narrative by describing the liberation of Israel from slavery in Egypt and the formation of a new community shaped by laws and shared identity.

Other books continue this historical thread by recording the rise and fall of kingdoms, the decisions of leaders, and the events that shaped the life of the nation. Books such as Kings or Chronicles document political developments across long stretches of time, describing alliances, wars, reforms, and moments of national crisis. The prophetic books approach history from another angle, speaking with urgency about justice, faithfulness, and the consequences of human decisions — often warning of danger while also offering hope for renewal.

Against this background, the book of Psalms stands apart. Instead of presenting a continuous storyline or a chronological account of events, Psalms gathers together a large collection of poems, prayers, and songs written at different moments and for different purposes. Each psalm functions as a self-contained expression of reflection or devotion. Some celebrate moments of joy or deliverance. Others express sorrow, frustration, or longing for justice. Still others offer quiet words of trust and gratitude.

Because of this structure, readers experience the Psalms differently from narrative books. Rather than following a story from beginning to end, the reader encounters a series of individual voices speaking from particular situations. One psalm may reflect deep distress, while the next celebrates God's power or faithfulness. The emotional tone can shift quickly because each poem reflects the experience of a different moment.

For this reason, many people approach the Psalms as a collection of individual passages rather than as a unified book. Over time, certain psalms become especially familiar and are associated with particular life experiences. Psalm 23 is often read during funerals because its imagery of a shepherd guiding and protecting a flock provides comfort in moments of grief. Psalm 51 appears frequently in contexts of confession, as it reflects a deep awareness of human failure and the desire for renewal. Psalm 121 is sometimes read during seasons of uncertainty, expressing confidence that help ultimately comes from God.

This pattern of reading is understandable — and it reflects the genuine power of individual psalms to speak into specific moments. But it can also create the impression that the Psalms are simply a loose collection of inspirational passages. When the book is approached only through familiar excerpts, it may appear fragmented or disconnected, as though the poems were gathered randomly without a larger structure or purpose.

In reality, the Psalms are far more carefully arranged than they might first appear. Although the individual psalms were written across many generations, the collection itself was eventually shaped and organized into a deliberate structure. The editors who preserved these writings did not simply place them together without thought. They arranged the psalms in a way that creates a broader reflection on faith, leadership, suffering, and hope — a reflection that becomes visible only when the book is approached as a whole.

Understanding this structure helps readers move beyond seeing the Psalms as isolated prayers and begin to recognize them as a thoughtfully composed book within the Bible. That recognition provides an important starting point for everything that follows.

A Collection That Developed Over Time

Another feature that distinguishes the Psalms from many other biblical books is the way the collection developed gradually over a long period of history. Unlike writings produced by a single author or during a brief historical window, the Psalms emerged through the contributions of many individuals who lived in different generations and faced very different circumstances.

Some of the earliest psalms appear to have been written during the reign of King David, who ruled Israel in the tenth century BCE. Other psalms were likely composed long after David's lifetime. Periods of political instability, invasion, exile, and restoration each created situations that called for prayer, lament, and thanksgiving. During the Babylonian exile in the sixth century BCE, the people of Israel experienced the loss of their homeland and the destruction of the temple in Jerusalem — a trauma that reshaped the spiritual and cultural life of the community. Some psalms reflect the grief and longing of that period with unmistakable clarity. Later generations who returned to Jerusalem continued to compose and preserve psalms that expressed their hopes for renewal.

Because the Psalms emerged from such a wide range of historical settings, the book captures many different perspectives on faith. Some voices express confidence and celebration, reflecting moments of peace or prosperity. Other voices speak from places of hardship, confusion, or longing for justice. Rather than presenting a single perspective on spiritual life, the Psalms preserve the reflections of people who lived through many different circumstances — and who found, in each of those circumstances, reason to write.

Over time, these individual writings were preserved, shared in worship, and eventually gathered together into collections. As those collections grew, editors arranged them into the structure that now appears in the Bible. The final result is a book that reflects centuries of reflection, prayer, and communal memory.

The Five Books of Psalms

One of the most important structural features of the Psalms is the way the collection is divided into five major sections, sometimes referred to as the "five books" of the Psalter.

The structure appears as follows:

Book One — Psalms 1–41

Book Two — Psalms 42–72

Book Three — Psalms 73–89

Book Four — Psalms 90–106

Book Five — Psalms 107–150

Each section concludes with a brief expression of praise directed toward God. These concluding statements are called doxologies — words that glorify or honor God — and they function as markers that signal the end of one section and the beginning of another. Psalm 41, for example, concludes: *"Praise be to the Lord, the God of Israel, from everlasting to everlasting. Amen and Amen."* Similar statements appear at the end of Psalms 72, 89, and 106. The final psalm of the entire collection, Psalm 150, serves as a climactic expression of praise that brings the whole book to a close.

This five-part structure is widely recognized by scholars as intentional. Some interpreters have suggested that the arrangement mirrors the structure of the Torah — the first five books of the Bible: Genesis, Exodus, Leviticus, Numbers, and Deuteronomy. If that connection was intended, the Psalms may have been organized as a companion to the law, providing the prayers and songs through which Israel responded to the story of God's relationship with His people. The Torah tells what God did; the Psalms record how the people answered.

Whether or not that parallel was deliberate, the structure itself demonstrates that the Psalms were carefully shaped by those who preserved them. The book is not a random gathering of poems but a thoughtfully organized work built through generations of reflection.

Different Types of Psalms

Another important step in understanding the book is recognizing that the Psalms include several distinct types of writing. Although the poems share common concerns, they often follow recognizable patterns that reflect the situations in which they were composed.

Psalms of praise celebrate God's greatness and power, acknowledging His role as creator and ruler of the world. They often call others to join in worship, inviting communities to sing, rejoice, and express gratitude for God's faithfulness. Laments give voice to sorrow or distress — the writer describes a difficult situation and appeals to God for help. These are among the most emotionally honest passages in the Bible, because they acknowledge the reality of suffering without attempting to soften it. Psalms of thanksgiving reflect moments when a period of difficulty has passed; the writer looks back on hardship and expresses gratitude for the way circumstances changed.

Some psalms focus on wisdom, reflecting on righteous living and the consequences of human choices. These writings resemble the teachings found in the book of Proverbs, encouraging readers to consider how their actions shape the direction of their lives. Still others are known as royal psalms, relating to the kingship of Israel and the role of the king as a representative of God's authority among the people.

Recognizing these categories helps explain why the Psalms move through such a wide range of emotions and perspectives. A reader moving from Psalm 22 — a raw cry of abandonment — to Psalm 23 — a quiet declaration of trust — is not encountering contradiction. They are encountering the full range of what faith looks like in practice.

The Role of David

When readers explore the Psalms, they often notice that many of the poems are associated with the name of David. The titles that appear before certain psalms describe them as being written "of David" or "for David," and because of these references, many people assume that David wrote the entire book.

In reality, the collection includes writings from several different individuals and groups. Some psalms are attributed to the descendants of Korah, others to Asaph, and still others to anonymous authors whose names were not preserved. The Psalms were never a single person's project.

David's prominence within the collection, however, is not arbitrary. According to the biblical narrative, David was not only a king but also a skilled musician and poet whose life included moments of remarkable success as well as periods of personal failure, repentance, and restoration. That arc — triumph, collapse, and return — mirrors the emotional movement found throughout the Psalms. His story gave later readers a human face for the kind of faith the poems describe: not faith that avoids difficulty, but faith that passes through it and comes out speaking to God on the other side.

18

A Book of Worship

From their earliest use, the Psalms functioned as songs and prayers within the worship life of Israel. In the temple in Jerusalem, musicians and singers used these poems during ceremonies and festivals. Worship gatherings brought communities together to remember their history, express gratitude, and seek God's guidance.

As the Psalms were repeated in worship, they became deeply embedded in the life of the people. The words shaped how individuals prayed, how they interpreted their experiences, and how they understood their relationship with God. A person did not need to compose their own words for grief or praise or confession — the Psalms provided them. In this way, the book served both a personal and a communal role. Individuals could pray these words in moments of private reflection, while communities could sing them together during public gatherings. The Psalms became the shared language through which a nation expressed its faith.

That function has not entirely disappeared. Many congregations today still read or sing the Psalms as part of regular worship, continuing a practice that stretches back thousands of years.

Poetry as a Way of Understanding Life

Another reason the Psalms stand apart from many other books of the Bible is their use of poetry. Unlike narrative writing, which moves forward through events and actions, poetry focuses on reflection, imagery, and emotional expression. Rather than describing what happened step by step, it invites readers to consider what those experiences felt like and what they reveal about the deeper realities of life.

The psalmists used poetic language to capture experiences that ordinary description struggles to express. Through imagery and metaphor, they describe both the beauty and the fragility of human existence. A person may be compared to grass that flourishes for a time before fading. God's protection may be pictured as the shelter of a strong tower or the care of a shepherd guiding a flock through unfamiliar terrain.

These images are not meant to function as literal descriptions. They provide a way of thinking about life and faith through symbols that speak to the imagination as well as the intellect. That is why poetic language often carries multiple layers of meaning — and why readers in very different cultures and historical settings can continue to find insight within the same passages. The words were written in a particular historical context, yet the imagery remains flexible enough to speak to new circumstances. A person reading Psalm 23 in a hospital room is not misreading the poem. They are discovering one of its intended dimensions.

The Emotional Depth of the Psalms

Another important feature of the Psalms is the depth of emotion expressed throughout the collection. While some religious writings emphasize clarity of belief or careful instruction about doctrine, the Psalms focus on the emotional dimensions of faith. The writers do not present spiritual life as a purely intellectual exercise. They describe how belief interacts with the full range of human experience — joy, gratitude, frustration, fear, and longing all appear within the same book.

This emotional range can surprise readers who expect religious writings to present faith as calm and untroubled. The Psalms reveal something far more complex. Faith, as portrayed in these poems, develops within the realities of life. It grows through experiences that include both celebration and struggle. The psalmists do not attempt to hide the difficulties they encounter.

They bring those experiences into their prayers, and the prayers are richer for it.

This openness is one of the reasons the Psalms have remained meaningful across generations. Readers recognize their own emotions within the words of the psalmists because those emotions — fear, gratitude, longing, relief — have not changed. The circumstances differ; the inner life does not.

The Movement Within the Psalms

Although each psalm stands as an individual poem, many of them follow a recognizable internal movement. A psalm may begin with a description of distress or uncertainty before gradually shifting toward trust, praise, or hope. This pattern reflects the way human reflection often unfolds — not in a straight line, but through a process of working something out.

The transition from distress to trust within a psalm does not necessarily imply that the external situation has changed. Instead, it reflects what happens when a person brings their experience honestly before God. The act of prayer itself becomes a place where perspective shifts. A poem might open with a description of enemies closing in and conclude with a declaration of confidence — not because the enemies have left, but because the writer has moved through something in the act of speaking.

For modern readers, recognizing this movement helps clarify how the Psalms function. These poems are not static declarations of belief. They are records of reflection in motion — faith working itself out in real time. That quality makes them companions for the reader's own process, not just finished products to admire.

The Psalms in the Life of Faith

Throughout history, the Psalms have played an important role in shaping how communities understand prayer and worship. From ancient Israel to modern congregations around the world, these poems have provided language for expressing faith across a wide variety of circumstances — in moments of national celebration and personal grief, in times of relative peace and seasons of profound uncertainty.

This ongoing use of the Psalms reflects their remarkable adaptability. The poems address themes that remain relevant in every generation: gratitude for life's blessings, concern for justice, the search for meaning in the midst of uncertainty. Because they speak to these concerns through poetry rather than argument, they remain open to new readers finding new dimensions within them. A psalm that once seemed abstract may take on new significance during a season of difficulty. Another that once felt simple may reveal a deeper meaning when viewed from a different stage of life.

In this way, the Psalms continue to function not only as historical documents but as living companions — texts that meet readers where they are rather than requiring them to come to the text already equipped.

Preparing to Understand the Psalms

Recognizing these features of the Psalms provides a foundation for deeper engagement with the book. Understanding that the collection developed gradually, that it includes many different types of writing, that it served a living worship community, and that it functions through poetic reflection rather than argument — these realities together help readers approach the text with greater awareness and realistic expectations.

Rather than expecting the Psalms to behave like a narrative story or a systematic explanation of belief, readers can appreciate them as expressions of faith shaped by real experiences across many generations. The poems do not offer immediate solutions. They invite readers into a process of reflection that unfolds over time — sometimes over a lifetime of returning to the same passages and finding that they have something new to say.

The book becomes, in this light, not merely a collection of familiar passages but a carefully shaped anthology of voices speaking across centuries. Those voices reflect the spiritual journey of a community that sought to understand life in relationship with God — and trusted that the search itself was worth preserving.

In the next chapter, we will step into the world that produced these poems. The cultural and social realities of ancient Israel shaped the experiences that gave rise to the Psalms, and understanding that world reveals why these writings took the particular form they did — and why that form has proven so durable.

Orientation for Modern Readers

The book of Psalms is not simply a collection of inspirational passages meant for occasional encouragement. It is a carefully preserved anthology of prayers and songs that developed over centuries, shaped by real historical circumstances, and eventually organized into a structured book that sits at the center of the Bible.

Recognizing this background allows readers to approach the Psalms with greater clarity. Each poem carries its own meaning, yet together they form a broader reflection on faith, suffering, leadership, justice, and hope. The individual psalm and the larger book are both worth attending to — and attending to one enriches the experience of the other.

Understanding the structure and development of the Psalms also helps explain why the book continues to resonate across generations. The voices preserved in these poems speak from real experiences that remain recognizable even today — not because the ancient world and the modern world are the same, but because the questions people bring to both have never fundamentally changed.

Chapter 3

The World Behind the Book

*"Lord, you have been our dwelling place throughout all generations.
Before the mountains were born or you brought forth the whole
world, from everlasting to everlasting you are God."*
— *Psalm 90:1–2*

Life in Ancient Israel

Understanding the book of Psalms becomes easier when readers
step back and consider the historical world in which these writings
first emerged. Although the emotions expressed in the Psalms
remain familiar to modern readers, the cultural and social
environment that shaped the poems was very different from the
world most people experience today. Ancient Israel existed within
a landscape defined by agriculture, tribal identity, political
instability, and a deep awareness of God's presence in everyday
life. Communities were smaller, communication moved slowly,
and the rhythms of existence were closely tied to seasons of
planting, harvest, and travel.

In such a world, people experienced life in ways that often
felt immediate and vulnerable. Drought could threaten survival.
Warfare between neighboring kingdoms could disrupt entire
regions. Disease, famine, or displacement could reshape
communities within a short period of time. Because many aspects
of life felt beyond human control, individuals and communities
frequently turned to prayer, worship, and reflection as ways of
understanding what they were experiencing.

The Psalms emerged from this environment. They reflect the
realities of people who believed that God was actively involved in

the unfolding of history and in the lives of individuals. For the writers of the Psalms, events such as victory in battle, the arrival of rain, the birth of children, or the restoration of peace were not merely natural occurrences — they were interpreted as signs of divine presence and guidance. At the same time, moments of suffering, injustice, or national crisis raised difficult questions about how God's purposes were being worked out in the world.

Because of this worldview, the language of the Psalms often connects ordinary events with spiritual meaning. The writers describe mountains, rivers, storms, and stars not simply as elements of the natural world but as reminders of God's creative power and authority. Human experiences — joy, fear, grief, and hope — are presented within a framework that assumes God remains attentive to the lives of His people.

Daily Life and the Rhythms of the Land

To understand the emotional tone of many psalms, it helps to consider the rhythms of daily life more closely. Unlike modern societies that rely heavily on technology and global systems of trade, most people in ancient Israel lived in small agricultural communities. Their lives were closely connected to the land, the seasons, and the natural patterns that governed planting and harvest.

Rainfall was one of the most important factors affecting survival. A season of sufficient rain could mean abundant crops and stability for families and villages. A prolonged drought could lead to famine and hardship. Because of this dependence on natural cycles, the arrival of rain or the failure of crops was rarely viewed as a purely natural occurrence. Such events were interpreted through a spiritual lens — people asked how these circumstances related to their relationship with God.

This connection between daily life and spiritual reflection appears throughout the Psalms. The writers refer to fertile fields, flowing water, storms, mountains, and deserts not as background scenery but as symbols of deeper realities. A tree planted beside a stream becomes an image of stability and flourishing. Parched ground becomes a metaphor for spiritual longing. The arrival of rain becomes a reminder of divine provision. For people whose survival depended directly on the rhythms of nature, this imagery carried immediate weight. The language of the Psalms reflects a world in which spiritual reflection and everyday experience were not separate concerns — they were the same concern, approached from different angles.

Travel also played an important role in shaping life. While most people lived in small villages, periodic journeys brought them into contact with larger gatherings of the community. Pilgrimages to Jerusalem during major festivals allowed individuals from many regions to gather together in worship. These journeys could be long and physically demanding, often involving travel across hills and valleys under difficult conditions.

Several psalms appear to have been associated with these journeys. The group of writings known as the "Songs of Ascents" (Psalms 120–134) may have been sung by pilgrims traveling toward Jerusalem. The language of these psalms reflects the experience of movement and anticipation as worshipers approached the city where the temple stood. Understanding this aspect of life explains why themes of journey, guidance, and protection appear repeatedly in the Psalms. Travel exposed individuals to danger from weather, terrain, and hostile groups. In such circumstances, prayer for safe arrival was not a formality — it was a genuine expression of dependence.

The Temple and the Life of Worship

A central feature of religious life in ancient Israel was the temple in Jerusalem. According to biblical tradition, the temple served as the primary location for worship, sacrifice, and communal gatherings that brought the nation together before God. Festivals held at the temple marked important moments in the calendar year and reminded the people of key events in their history.

Within this setting, music played an essential role. Worship was not limited to spoken prayers or sacrificial rituals. Songs, instruments, and choral responses were woven into the ceremonies that took place during temple gatherings. The Psalms were deeply connected to this environment, serving as songs that could be sung by individuals, choirs, or entire communities.

Historical passages elsewhere in the Bible describe groups of musicians and singers who were appointed to assist with worship in the temple. These individuals often belonged to families or clans dedicated to this responsibility. Their task involved learning the words of the psalms, mastering musical arrangements, and leading the people in expressions of praise or lament. Through repeated use in worship, the Psalms became familiar to the broader population. A person might hear the same psalm during different festivals or gatherings, gradually associating its words with particular memories and experiences. Over time, the Psalms formed a shared language that helped communities express their faith collectively.

This connection with worship also explains why many psalms invite others to join in praise. Passages that begin with phrases such as "Sing to the Lord," "Praise the Lord," or "Give thanks to the Lord" were likely intended to encourage communal participation. These were not personal reflections that happened to be preserved — they were designed to guide the worship of the entire nation.

The Monarchy and the Legacy of David

Another important aspect of the historical world behind the Psalms involves the monarchy of Israel, particularly the reign of King David. According to the biblical narrative, David ruled Israel during a period when the nation achieved relative stability and unity. His leadership established Jerusalem as the political and spiritual center of the kingdom.

David is frequently associated with the Psalms, not only because several psalms bear his name but also because his life story reflects many of the emotional themes present within the collection. The biblical accounts describe David as both a warrior and a musician — someone who experienced dramatic victories as well as personal failures and deep moments of repentance. These experiences mirror the emotional range found in the Psalms. Some psalms celebrate triumph and confidence. Others express remorse, humility, or longing for forgiveness.

Whether David personally wrote every psalm attributed to him remains a topic of scholarly discussion. What is clear is that his life became symbolic of the broader spiritual journey of Israel. His story provided a framework through which later generations could reflect on themes such as leadership, repentance, and trust in God — and it gave the collection a human face that readers could recognize as their own.

Crisis and Exile

While some psalms reflect times of stability and celebration, others clearly emerge from moments of national crisis. Throughout its history, Israel experienced periods when foreign powers threatened its independence or forced its people into exile. One of the most significant of these moments occurred in the sixth century BCE, when the Babylonian Empire conquered Jerusalem and carried many of the inhabitants away from their homeland.

The experience of exile was deeply traumatic. The temple was destroyed, the monarchy collapsed, and the people were forced to live in a foreign land. For many Israelites, these events raised painful questions about their identity and their relationship with

God. If the nation had been chosen by God, how could such a disaster have occurred?

Several psalms appear to reflect the emotional weight of this period — speaking of longing for restoration, remembering the past, and hoping for a future in which the people might once again return to their homeland. The language of grief found in these psalms demonstrates how the community processed its collective suffering through prayer and song. Even after the exile ended and some people returned to Jerusalem, the memory of those events continued to shape the identity of the nation. The Psalms preserved the emotional record of that experience, allowing later generations to remember both the pain of loss and the possibility of restoration.

Memory and Story

The Psalms frequently refer to events from Israel's history, reminding readers of moments when God acted on behalf of His people. Stories of deliverance, guidance, and provision were not simply historical recollections — they served as reminders that the present moment was part of a larger narrative.

Several psalms recount the story of the exodus from Egypt, when the Israelites believed God rescued them from slavery and led them toward a new land. Others recall the wilderness journey, the establishment of the kingdom, or the rebuilding of Jerusalem after exile. By revisiting these stories, the psalmists reinforced the belief that God remained faithful throughout changing circumstances. The past became a source of encouragement during difficult times. If God had acted before, there was reason to believe He could act again.

This emphasis on memory also helped maintain continuity across generations. Parents and teachers passed these stories along to their children, ensuring that the lessons of the past continued to shape the future. Memory, in the Psalms, is never simply nostalgia.

It is a form of argument — evidence drawn from history in support of present hope.

Education and the Transmission of Tradition

The world behind the Psalms also included systems through which traditions and teachings were passed from one generation to the next. Because written texts were less widely available than they are today, memory and oral tradition played a significant role in preserving important ideas and stories.

Families and community leaders often taught younger generations through storytelling, recitation, and song. The Psalms, with their poetic structure and repeated imagery, were particularly suited to this form of transmission. Their rhythm and parallel structure made them easier to remember and repeat. Through this process, the Psalms became part of the cultural memory of the people. Children grew up hearing these songs and prayers, learning the language of faith from an early age. As they matured, they continued to encounter the same psalms in worship and reflection, deepening their understanding over time.

This pattern of transmission explains why the Psalms frequently emphasize remembering and teaching. Several passages encourage the community to recount God's actions in the past so that future generations will understand their identity and purpose. The Psalms functioned not only as expressions of personal devotion but as tools for shaping the spiritual imagination of the community — a form of education that happened not in classrooms but in worship, in homes, and on the road to Jerusalem.

Leadership and Justice

Life in ancient Israel was also shaped by persistent questions of leadership and justice. The nation existed within a region where political power shifted frequently as kingdoms rose and fell. Neighboring nations sometimes formed alliances, while at other times they engaged in warfare that affected entire populations.

Within this environment, the character of leadership carried significant importance. Kings were expected not only to provide military protection but also to uphold justice and ensure stability within the community. When leaders acted with wisdom and fairness, society could flourish. When leadership failed, the consequences fell hardest on the most vulnerable members of the population.

The Psalms reflect these concerns directly. Some psalms celebrate the role of the king as a representative of God's authority, asking that the ruler govern with wisdom and integrity. Others express sharp concern about injustice — describing situations in which the powerful exploit the weak or disregard the needs of the poor. These reflections reveal how closely spiritual life and social responsibility were connected in ancient Israel. Faith was not limited to private belief; it was expected to shape how communities treated one another. Justice, compassion, and humility were not civic virtues separate from religion — they were expressions of faithfulness to God.

The Experience of Vulnerability

Another factor shaping the world of the Psalms was the vulnerability experienced by individuals and communities. Ancient societies lacked many of the systems that provide stability in the modern world. There were no advanced medical treatments for disease, no centralized systems of emergency assistance, and limited means of communication across long distances.

As a result, life could change dramatically in a short period of time. Illness could spread through a community with little warning. Crops could fail after months of labor. Political conflicts could disrupt entire regions. These realities contributed to a strong awareness of dependence — people recognized that many aspects of life remained beyond human control. In such circumstances, prayer and worship provided ways of expressing both gratitude and need.

The Psalms capture this sense of vulnerability directly. Some poems describe situations in which the writer feels surrounded by enemies or threatened by circumstances that seem impossible to resolve. Others speak of illness or weakness, acknowledging the fragility of human life. Yet even within these expressions of vulnerability, the writers turn toward hope. The psalmists repeatedly affirm that God remains attentive to the needs of His people — a conviction that provides a foundation for trust precisely when external circumstances give little reason for it.

The Role of Poetry

Another aspect of the world behind the Psalms involves the literary form in which they were written. Hebrew poetry differs from modern Western poetry in several important ways. Instead of relying primarily on rhyme or fixed rhythm, Hebrew poetry often emphasizes parallelism — a technique in which ideas are repeated or expanded through closely related lines.

A line might express an idea, and the following line will restate that idea using slightly different language. This structure reinforces the meaning of the poem while allowing the writer to explore the idea from multiple angles. It also slows the reader down. Where prose moves forward, parallelism circles back — it insists that the idea be held a moment longer, turned over, considered again from a slightly different angle.

Because of this poetic style, the Psalms often feel reflective and layered in ways that resist quick reading. That quality was not incidental. The structure also made the psalms easier to remember when they were sung or recited in worship — the repetition served both as artistic form and as a practical aid to memorization.

The Natural World as a Source of Reflection

Another important element of the historical world behind the Psalms is the way the natural environment influenced spiritual reflection. The landscape of ancient Israel included mountains, valleys, deserts, rivers, and fertile plains. Each of these settings provided imagery that the psalmists used to express deeper ideas about life and faith.

The landscape itself carried meaning. Mountains suggested endurance and long-standing stability. Flowing water pointed to life, provision, and renewal in an otherwise dry land. The desert became a place of testing — where hardship exposed dependence and shaped resilience. The psalmists drew on these images consistently to describe spiritual realities. God's protection might be compared to the shelter of a mountain. Spiritual longing might be described as thirst in a dry land. The joy of restoration might be likened to fields flourishing after rain.

For people living in this environment, such imagery felt immediate and vivid. For readers today, it remains compelling for a different reason: these images connect spiritual ideas with physical experiences that remain universally recognizable regardless of time or place. The psalmists wrote in a particular landscape, but they were reaching for something that landscape could only partially contain.

Continuity and Change

Although the historical setting of the Psalms may feel distant from the modern world, the underlying human experiences described in the poems remain deeply familiar. People today still encounter uncertainty, loss, gratitude, and hope. Communities continue to wrestle with questions of justice, leadership, and identity. The cultural forms through which these experiences are expressed may differ, yet the emotional and spiritual questions remain remarkably consistent across centuries.

Understanding the historical world behind the Psalms does more than provide background information. It helps readers see how ancient individuals responded to circumstances that in many ways resemble the challenges people face today. The psalmists lived in a world shaped by different technologies and social structures, yet they wrestled with the same fundamental questions: How should one respond to suffering? Where can hope be found during uncertainty? How can gratitude be expressed when life brings unexpected blessing? How can faith be maintained when institutions fail and the future is unclear?

These are not ancient questions that happen to have modern echoes. They are human questions — the kind that surface in every generation, in every culture, as long as people live in a world they do not fully control.

By examining the historical context of these writings, readers gain a deeper appreciation for the voices preserved within the Psalms. These poems represent generations of reflection shaped by the realities of life in ancient Israel — and they continue to speak across centuries because the experiences they describe remain part of the shared human story.

With this historical background in mind, we are now prepared to examine the structure and flow of the book itself. In the next chapter, we will explore how the Psalms are arranged within the Bible and how the sequence of the collection reveals patterns that help readers understand the larger message of the book.

Chapter 4

The Story or Flow of the Book

"I will open my mouth with a parable; I will utter hidden things, things from of old — things we have heard and known, things our ancestors have told us. We will not hide them from their descendants; we will tell the next generation the praiseworthy deeds of the Lord."
— Psalm 78:2–4

Understanding the Structure of the Psalms

Unlike many other books of the Bible, the book of Psalms does not unfold as a continuous narrative. There are no central characters whose lives move forward chapter by chapter, and there are no events that develop in a chronological storyline. Instead, the Psalms consist of a collection of poems, prayers, and songs written across many generations.

Because of this, readers sometimes struggle to understand how the book fits together as a whole. When someone first opens the Psalms, it can appear to be simply a gathering of unrelated spiritual reflections placed side by side without any clear connection between them. One psalm may celebrate joy and gratitude, while the next expresses grief or frustration. Another might reflect on the beauty of creation or the pursuit of wisdom.

At first glance, this variety can make the book seem fragmented. Yet when the Psalms are examined more closely, a deeper structure begins to emerge. The book may not tell a single narrative, but it does reflect a larger pattern shaped by the spiritual experiences of the people who wrote and preserved these poems.

Rather than following a storyline of events, the Psalms trace the movement of human experience in relationship with God. The writers describe moments of celebration and renewal, but they also record seasons of uncertainty, hardship, and longing. Taken together, these reflections reveal a portrait of faith that includes both confidence and questioning — and the structure of the book reflects that range deliberately.

This is worth pausing on, because it reshapes how a reader might approach the book. Most collections are organized by topic, chronology, or author. The Psalms are organized by something harder to name — something closer to the rhythm of a lived spiritual life. Seasons of confidence appear alongside seasons of doubt. Poems of corporate celebration sit beside poems of intensely personal crisis. The editors who shaped the final collection were not trying to resolve those contrasts. They were trying to preserve them, because they understood that a community of faith needs language for all of it.

As introduced in Chapter 2, the collection is divided into five sections, each concluding with a doxology — a brief expression of praise that marks the end of one book and the beginning of another. That five-part framework is the skeleton. This chapter is concerned with the living movement within it: how the Psalms flow, how they were used, and what the overall shape of the collection reveals about the nature of faith.

The Psalms in Israel's Worship

The Psalms were not written to sit on a page. They were spoken, sung, and repeated within the life of a community. Understanding how they functioned in worship is essential to understanding why they are arranged as they are.

Worship in ancient Israel was not a private activity. It involved the gathered people. Music, recitation, and communal response allowed individuals to participate together rather than remain isolated in their experiences. The temple in Jerusalem served as the center of this activity, especially during festivals and significant moments in the life of the nation. Within that setting, the Psalms gave voice to what people often struggled to express on their own — words for gratitude when blessings were clear, words for grief when loss was overwhelming, words for trust when circumstances were uncertain.

Rather than separating people by their individual situations, the Psalms brought those experiences into a shared space. One person's lament could become the community's prayer. One person's praise could become the community's declaration. This is part of why the collection includes such a wide range of emotional expression within a single book. The Psalms were not arranged to reflect one kind of moment — they were arranged to serve every kind of moment that a worshiping community might face across generations.

Different psalms were used in different settings. Some were associated with national celebrations or moments of military victory. Others appear to have been connected with repentance, mourning, or crisis. Certain psalms may have been used in royal ceremonies, while others were intended for the regular rhythms of communal worship.

A vivid example appears in the "Songs of Ascents" (Psalms 120–134). These psalms are strongly associated with the pilgrimages people made to Jerusalem for major festivals. As individuals and families traveled toward the city — often across several days of difficult terrain — these songs would have shaped their focus and prepared their hearts for worship. The psalms in this group have a particular quality of movement and anticipation, a sense of drawing near to something. They were functional in the most literal sense: designed to be carried on a journey and sung along the way.

Other psalms include instructions related to music, instruments, or leadership. References to choirs, directors, and specific instruments suggest that organized groups played a role in guiding communal participation. Worship was structured, but it was also participatory — the Psalms were not performed for the people but sung by them.

These details point toward a larger reality. The Psalms were embedded in daily and seasonal life in ways that shaped how people understood their own experiences. The language of the Psalms became the language of the people — the vocabulary through which generations of Israelites named what they felt and brought it before God.

From Individual Prayer to Community Worship

Although many psalms were used within communal gatherings, the tone of the poems often remains deeply personal. The writers frequently speak about their own fears, hopes, disappointments, and moments of gratitude. A psalm might describe the writer's sense of distress during a time of danger or illness. Another might celebrate the relief that follows a period of uncertainty.

Yet even these personal reflections became part of the shared worship life of the community. When individuals gathered to sing or recite these psalms, the words of one person resonated with the experiences of many others. Someone who felt overwhelmed by hardship might recognize their own emotions in a psalm written centuries earlier. Another person celebrating a moment of restoration might find language for gratitude within a different psalm.

This blending of personal and communal reflection became one of the defining characteristics of the Psalter. Individual voices were preserved, but those voices also invited participation from the entire community. Through this process, the Psalms became both personal prayers and shared expressions of faith — allowing individuals to speak honestly about their experiences while reminding them that they were part of a larger community shaped by similar struggles and hopes.

40

This is why the Psalms have retained their usefulness across such different contexts. A psalm composed in a moment of personal crisis in ancient Israel can function just as powerfully in a congregation of modern worshipers who have never faced the same specific circumstances — because the emotional and spiritual movement within the poem is recognizable regardless of the particulars that prompted it.

A Journey Through Different Expressions of Faith

Although the Psalms do not follow a chronological storyline, the collection can be understood as a kind of spiritual journey. As readers move through the book, they encounter a wide range of emotional and spiritual experiences — deep confidence in God's guidance, gratitude after deliverance, confusion about why injustice appears to prevail, quiet trust in the midst of unresolved difficulty.

These contrasting perspectives mirror the complexity of human life. Faith is rarely experienced as a single, unchanging emotion. Instead, individuals move through seasons of joy, uncertainty, frustration, and renewal — sometimes within the same week, sometimes within the same day. The Psalms preserve each of these experiences without attempting to eliminate the tension between them. A psalm of lament may appear next to a psalm of praise not because the editors were careless but because both represent authentic responses to life, and life does not organize itself by category.

This arrangement also serves a pastoral purpose. A reader who comes to the Psalms during a season of grief does not need to search through a section labeled "lament" to find language that fits. The range of human experience is woven throughout the collection, which means that wherever a reader enters the book, they are likely to find something that speaks to where they actually are. The diversity within the Psalms is not a problem to be explained away — it is a feature that makes the book usable across every season of life.

In this way, the book functions almost like a map of the human spiritual journey. The psalmists record moments when they feel close to God as well as moments when that relationship feels distant or strained. By preserving these reflections together, the Psalms remind readers that faith develops over time — not in a straight line, but through experiences that challenge, refine, and deepen understanding. The collection as a whole communicates something that no individual psalm could communicate alone: that the full range of human experience belongs within a life of faith, and that God remains the addressee throughout all of it.

The Movement Toward Praise

One of the most significant patterns within the Psalms becomes visible only when the book is viewed as a whole. While many of the earlier psalms contain expressions of distress or questioning, the closing portion of the Psalter shifts increasingly toward praise. The movement is gradual and not without disruption — lament does not disappear in the later books — but the overall arc is unmistakable.

The final psalms in the collection celebrate God's greatness and invite the entire community to respond with worship. Instruments, voices, and joyful expressions of gratitude appear repeatedly in these concluding poems. Psalm 150, which brings the entire book to a close, calls for praise using every available instrument and voice. It is an explosion of worship that draws every element of creation into participation.

This ending does not erase the struggles described earlier in the book. Psalm 150 does not pretend that Psalm 88 — one of the darkest and most unresolved laments in the entire collection — did not happen. Psalm 88 ends without resolution, without a turn toward hope, without even the customary closing affirmation of trust. It simply stops in the darkness. The Psalter preserves that poem without softening it. And then it continues — through more lament, more praise, more questioning — and eventually arrives at Psalm 150.

That sequence matters. The movement from honest struggle to genuine praise is real in the Psalms, but it is never presented as quick or easy. The book earns its ending. By the time readers reach the final doxology, they have traveled through the full range of what faith looks like in practice — the confidence, the confusion, the waiting, the grief, and the gratitude. The final praise does not dismiss what came before. It encompasses it.

For readers who engage the Psalms as a whole rather than in fragments, this arc becomes one of the most meaningful features of the book. It models something important about the nature of faith: that the path from honest struggle to genuine praise is real, even when it is long, and that arriving at worship having passed through difficulty is not a lesser form of praise but perhaps the deepest form of it.

The Psalms as a Guide for Prayer

In addition to their role in communal worship, the Psalms have long served as a guide for personal prayer. Because the collection expresses such a wide range of emotions and experiences, many readers have found that the Psalms provide language for moments when their own words fall short.

Throughout history, individuals have turned to the Psalms during times of grief, celebration, uncertainty, or gratitude. The poems offer expressions that resonate with experiences people encounter across every stage of life. Someone facing a difficult season may find comfort in a psalm that acknowledges distress while still expressing hope. Another person celebrating a moment of renewal may discover that the words of praise in the Psalter capture their sense of gratitude more fully than anything they could compose themselves.

This ability to provide language for prayer is one reason the Psalms have remained central to spiritual practice across so many different traditions. The book does not ask readers to observe its expressions from a distance — it invites them in. The first-person voice that runs through so many psalms creates a sense of immediacy that other forms of religious writing often lack. When a psalmist writes "my soul thirsts for you" or "how long, Lord?" the words are not presented as someone else's experience to be studied but as a template that readers are invited to inhabit.

This quality helps explain why so many people find that the Psalms pray for them in moments when they cannot pray for themselves. Grief can make language difficult. Crisis can reduce a person to silence. In those moments, the Psalms offer something already formed — words that have already done the work of giving shape to what would otherwise remain unspoken. By praying or reflecting on the words of the Psalms, individuals join a conversation that has continued for thousands of years, participating in the same pattern of response that has shaped communities of faith across generations.

Seeing the Psalms as a Whole

When readers first encounter the Psalms, the book may appear to be a collection of unrelated poems. Yet when its structure and purpose are understood, a deeper pattern becomes visible.

The five-book arrangement provides the organizing framework. The connection to Israel's worship practices reveals how these poems functioned within the life of the community — not as texts to be studied but as words to be spoken and sung within the rhythms of real life. The blending of personal and communal reflection demonstrates how individual experiences became shared expressions of faith that could carry meaning for people who had never lived through the same specific circumstances. And the overall movement of the collection — from the wisdom of Psalm 1 through lament and praise and crisis and restoration, arriving finally at the full-throated celebration of Psalm 150 — reveals a shape that mirrors the shape of a faithful life: honest, persistent, and ultimately oriented toward gratitude.

Together, these elements show that the Psalms form more than a collection of isolated prayers. They represent a record of spiritual reflection that developed across centuries as individuals and communities sought to understand their lives in relationship with God. Each poem contributes to a larger conversation about faith, struggle, gratitude, and hope — a conversation that the Psalms do not conclude so much as hold open, inviting each new generation of readers to bring their own experience into it.

The flow of the Psalms mirrors the rhythms of life itself. Moments of sorrow are followed by renewal. Questions give way to insight. Struggles eventually lead toward hope — not because the Psalms promise that every difficulty will resolve quickly, but because the collection as a whole demonstrates that people have always found their way through, and have found in that passage reason to praise.

The Psalter preserves these experiences so that future readers can recognize their own lives within the same pattern. Through poetry, prayer, and honest reflection, the Psalms continue to guide individuals and communities as they seek meaning, faith, and hope in every season of life. The flow of the book is not defined by chronological events. It is defined by the shared experiences of people who sought to express their relationship with God through the full range of what it means to be human — and who trusted that bringing that full range before God was itself an act of faith worth preserving.

Chapter 5

Key Themes

*"The Lord is my shepherd, I lack nothing. He makes me lie down
in green pastures, he leads me beside quiet waters, he refreshes my
soul."*
— Psalm 23:1–3

The Voice of Worship and Praise

One of the most visible themes running throughout the Psalms is
the practice of praise. Many of the poems celebrate God's
greatness, inviting individuals and communities to recognize His
power, wisdom, and presence within the world. These expressions
of praise appear in a variety of forms — sometimes emerging as
joyful songs sung in public worship and at other times appearing
as quiet reflections offered by individuals who have experienced a
moment of gratitude.

Praise in the Psalms is not limited to simple statements of
admiration. Instead, it often includes vivid descriptions of God's
activity in the world. The writers reflect on the beauty of creation,
the movement of the stars, the strength of mountains, and the
rhythms of the seasons. These images remind readers that the
natural world itself can be understood as evidence of divine
creativity and care.

An important dimension of this praise is the idea that it
functions as a response to what God has already done. Many
psalms describe specific moments in which the writer believes that
God has acted within a situation — bringing protection, healing,
guidance, or restoration. The psalmist does not simply
acknowledge the change in circumstances but responds with

gratitude expressed through song or prayer. A psalm may begin by recounting a time of danger or distress, then recall how the situation changed, and conclude with an invitation to praise God for the help that was received. Through this structure, the psalmists demonstrate how gratitude becomes an essential element of spiritual life. Praise becomes a way of remembering — acknowledging that life's positive developments are not taken for granted and that the one who provided them deserves to be named.

Yet the Psalms do not present praise as something limited to moments of celebration or resolved difficulty. Many poems invite readers to praise God even when circumstances remain uncertain. This approach suggests that worship is not only a response to favorable situations but also a way of maintaining orientation during seasons when answers are not immediately visible. The psalmists sometimes choose to celebrate God's faithfulness even before their situation has changed — affirming that their hope does not depend entirely on current conditions. Trust and praise, in the Psalms, are not sequential. They are intertwined.

Although many psalms arise from personal experience, the language of praise frequently expands beyond the individual writer. Phrases such as "Sing to the Lord," "Give thanks to the Lord," or "Let all the earth rejoice" appear repeatedly throughout the book. These invitations suggest that praise was meant to be shared rather than experienced in isolation. When individuals gathered for worship at the temple, the words of the Psalms allowed them to express gratitude together — affirming their shared identity and their common trust in God. Through repeated communal use, the language of the Psalms became the language of the people.

Many psalms also expand the invitation beyond human voices entirely, calling the natural world itself to participate in worship. Rivers are described as clapping their hands, mountains as singing for joy, and the heavens as declaring the glory of God. These poetic images do not suggest that nature literally speaks in human language. Instead, they communicate the idea that creation itself reflects the presence and power of its Creator — that worship extends beyond the boundaries of human communities and that the entire universe becomes a stage on which God's creativity and authority are displayed.

Trust in the Midst of Uncertainty

Closely connected with praise is the theme of trust. The writers of the Psalms frequently describe God as a refuge, a fortress, or a source of protection during times of danger. These images reflect the realities of ancient life, when threats from enemies, natural disasters, or personal hardship could disrupt ordinary routines without warning.

The language of refuge appears repeatedly throughout the book. By comparing God to a stronghold or shelter, the psalmists communicate their belief that safety ultimately comes from divine care rather than human strength. This perspective allowed individuals to face uncertain circumstances with a measure of confidence, even when the outcome of a situation remained unclear.

Trust in the Psalms does not mean that the writers ignore the presence of danger. Many poems openly describe the threats surrounding the speaker — enemies who seek harm, illness that weakens the body, social injustice that undermines peace within the community. These descriptions make it clear that the psalmists are not detached from the realities of life. Instead of pretending that these challenges do not exist, the writers acknowledge them while expressing confidence that God remains attentive. Trust becomes an act of faith in the midst of uncertainty rather than a denial of difficulty. The psalmists recognize that circumstances may change, but they continue to believe that God's presence offers stability within those changes.

At times, the Psalms also address moments when God's presence seems difficult to perceive. Some writers describe periods in which their prayers appear unanswered, or their circumstances remain unchanged despite their appeals for help. Rather than avoiding the subject, the psalmists acknowledge the experience of waiting and uncertainty openly. They speak about feeling abandoned or forgotten, asking why relief has not yet arrived. Yet even within these moments of questioning, the writers continue to direct their words toward God. The act of prayer itself becomes a sign that faith has not disappeared. The psalmist may not understand what is happening, but the conversation with God continues.

This willingness to wrestle with silence demonstrates the depth of honesty present within the Psalms. Faith is portrayed not as a constant state of certainty but as a relationship that persists even when understanding remains incomplete. By preserving these voices of struggle alongside expressions of confident trust, the Psalms acknowledge the full range of what faith looks like across the seasons of a life.

This theme resonates with readers across generations because it reflects a familiar tension within human experience. Life often includes moments when answers remain unclear and outcomes remain uncertain. The Psalms suggest that faith involves choosing to trust even when clarity has not yet arrived — and that this choice, made repeatedly and honestly, is itself a form of devotion.

Lament and the Reality of Suffering

While praise and trust appear frequently in the Psalms, another major theme involves lament. A large portion of the book consists of poems that describe distress, grief, or frustration. These psalms demonstrate that faith does not eliminate suffering but instead provides a framework for expressing it honestly.

In lament psalms, the writer often begins by describing a difficult situation in specific and sometimes striking terms. The language may refer to enemies who threaten the speaker, illness that weakens the body, or injustice that disrupts the community. After describing the situation, the psalmist usually turns toward God with a request for help — asking for protection, healing, or justice, expressing a belief that God has the ability to intervene. This appeal transforms the poem from a simple expression of frustration into an act of prayer.

One of the most striking aspects of lament psalms is their honesty. The writers do not hide their emotions or soften their language. They speak openly about fear, confusion, and anger, bringing those feelings into their conversation with God. In doing so, the Psalms reveal that faith can coexist with deep emotional struggle — that there is no required composure before approaching God, no prerequisite of having sorted through one's feelings before they are permitted into prayer.

Many lament psalms eventually shift toward a declaration of trust or praise. Even when the difficult circumstances remain unresolved, the writer often concludes by expressing hope that God will respond. This movement from distress to trust reflects an internal process in which the speaker chooses to place confidence in God despite the surrounding uncertainty. But not every lament psalm makes that turn. Some end in the darkness, without resolution, without a closing affirmation of hope. The Psalms preserve those poems too — because honest faith sometimes means staying in the difficulty rather than resolving it prematurely. Through the full range of lament, the Psalms provide readers with language for confronting suffering without abandoning faith and without being required to perform a confidence they do not yet feel.

Justice and Righteousness

Another recurring theme throughout the Psalms involves the relationship between justice and righteousness. The writers frequently reflect on the difference between those who seek to live according to God's guidance and those who pursue selfish or destructive paths.

In many psalms, the righteous are described as individuals who trust in God, practice humility, and act with integrity toward others. Their lives are compared to trees planted near streams of water — stable, nourished, and producing fruit over time. The wicked, by contrast, are portrayed as people whose actions undermine the well-being of others and disrupt the moral order of society. These descriptions reflect the belief that God cares deeply about justice and that human behavior has consequences that extend beyond the individual into the community.

The psalmists repeatedly call on God to intervene when injustice appears to prevail — asking for protection from those who misuse power and for restoration when communities are harmed by corruption or violence. At the same time, the Psalms acknowledge that the relationship between righteousness and prosperity is not always straightforward. Some writers express open frustration when they see people who act unjustly yet appear to flourish. These moments of confusion reveal the tension between the ideal vision of justice and the observable realities of life. Rather than resolving that tension too quickly, the Psalms allow it to remain — inviting readers to wrestle with the complexity of moral experience alongside the writers.

This theme carries a particular relevance for modern readers. Questions about fairness, accountability, and the apparent success of those who act unjustly are not unique to ancient Israel. They surface in every generation. The Psalms do not offer easy answers, but they demonstrate that bringing those questions before God — honestly and persistently — is itself a form of faithfulness.

The Kingship of God

A theme that becomes increasingly prominent throughout the Psalms is the idea that God reigns as the ultimate king over the world. While human leaders play important roles within society, the psalmists emphasize that divine authority stands above all earthly power — and that no political collapse, no military defeat, and no institutional failure can undermine that authority.

Several psalms celebrate this kingship by describing God's rule over creation. The writers portray the seas, mountains, and skies as responding to God's command, illustrating the belief that the natural world operates under divine guidance. Other psalms connect God's kingship with the concept of justice — expressing hope that God's rule will bring fairness and restoration to a world often marked by inequality and suffering. This vision encourages readers to trust that injustice will not endure indefinitely, even when its end is not yet visible.

During periods when Israel experienced political instability or national crisis, the theme of God's kingship became especially meaningful. Even if human leaders failed or institutions collapsed, the psalmists continued to affirm that God's authority remained secure. This was not escapism — it was a source of resilience. Anchoring trust in an authority that transcends human political arrangements allowed the community to maintain coherence and hope in circumstances that might otherwise have produced only despair.

For modern readers, this theme offers a similar kind of grounding. The Psalms do not promise that human institutions will be just or stable. They promise something different — that behind and beyond those institutions, a larger authority remains in place, one that is oriented toward justice and capable of bringing restoration.

Hope and Restoration

Running beneath many of the Psalms, even in poems that begin with distress or lament, is a persistent current of hope. This hope does not depend solely on favorable circumstances. It arises from the belief that God continues to work within history — and from the memory of times when that work was unmistakably visible.

Some psalms recall earlier moments when the people experienced deliverance or restoration. By remembering these events, the writers reinforce the belief that present difficulties do not represent the final chapter of the story. If God acted before, there is reason to believe He can act again. Memory, in the Psalms, is never merely sentimental — it is argumentative. The psalmists reach into the past to find evidence for present hope, using what has already occurred as grounds for confidence in what has not yet arrived.

Other psalms look toward the future, anticipating a time when peace and justice will prevail more fully than they do now. These expressions of hope remind readers that faith often involves looking beyond immediate circumstances toward a larger vision of restoration. The horizon of the Psalms extends beyond any single moment, any single generation, any single set of circumstances. This long view is part of what has allowed the Psalms to remain meaningful across so many different eras — they were never written to speak only to the moment that produced them.

Themes That Intertwine

When the themes of praise, trust, lament, justice, kingship, and hope are considered together, they reveal how the Psalms operate as an interconnected work rather than a random collection of writings. Each theme appears repeatedly across different psalms, reinforcing the others and deepening the overall message of the book.

Praise reminds readers of God's greatness and creativity. Trust encourages confidence even when circumstances feel unstable. Lament provides language for confronting suffering without abandoning faith. Reflections on justice highlight the importance of righteousness within community life. The theme of God's kingship affirms that divine authority stands above human power. Hope points toward restoration beyond present hardship.

54

What is notable is that none of these themes operates in isolation. A psalm of praise may carry within it an undertone of lament. A psalm of trust may be saturated with the memory of past deliverance. A psalm of lament may conclude with an affirmation that God's kingship remains secure. The themes are not separate rooms in the same building — they are woven through every wall.

Together, these themes form the foundation of the Psalms' enduring influence. The poems do not attempt to simplify the complexities of life. Instead, they acknowledge those complexities while directing attention toward a relationship with God that encompasses every dimension of human experience. Understanding them prepares readers to engage the Psalms more deeply — recognizing not just what any individual poem is saying, but how it participates in a larger conversation that the book as a whole has been sustaining across centuries.

In the next chapter, we will examine how readers sometimes misunderstand the Psalms when they approach the book without considering its historical and literary context. Recognizing these common misunderstandings helps clarify how the Psalms are intended to function within the broader story of the Bible.

Chapter 6

Where People Get It Wrong

*"Why, Lord, do you stand far off? Why do you hide yourself in
times of trouble?"*
— Psalm 10:1

Reading the Psalms as Isolated Verses

One of the most common ways readers misunderstand the book
of Psalms is by approaching it only as a collection of individual
verses or short passages that offer encouragement during difficult
moments. Many people become familiar with a handful of well-
known psalms — Psalm 23, Psalm 121, Psalm 46 — and return to
those passages whenever they are seeking comfort or reassurance.
While this approach can provide genuine encouragement, it also
leads readers to overlook the broader context in which the Psalms
were written, and to miss much of what makes those familiar
passages powerful in the first place.

The Psalms were not originally intended to function as
isolated quotations. Each psalm was composed as a complete
poem expressing a particular experience or reflection, and the
collection itself was arranged in a deliberate structure that reflects
the spiritual journey of a community across generations. When
readers focus only on individual lines, they miss the larger
movement of thought that gives the psalm its meaning.

A lament psalm often begins with a description of distress
before gradually moving toward trust or praise. If only the closing
lines are remembered, the reader misses the emotional struggle
that led to that expression of confidence — and misses, therefore,
the reason the confidence is hard-won and worth noting.

Likewise, a psalm of praise may draw its power from earlier references to hardship or deliverance that explain why gratitude is being expressed. Read without that context, the praise can feel generic. Read with it, the praise feels earned.

Understanding the Psalms requires reading each poem as a complete piece of writing and recognizing how it fits within the larger structure of the book. This does not mean that a single verse can never provide comfort on its own — clearly it can. But the verse will mean more, not less, when the reader also knows the poem it comes from, and the journey it represents.

Expecting the Psalms to Offer Simple Answers

Another misunderstanding arises when readers expect the Psalms to provide straightforward solutions to every difficulty they encounter. Because the book contains many expressions of trust and praise, some readers assume that faith should always lead quickly to peace or certainty — that the movement from lament to confidence should be swift, and that a faith that struggles is somehow deficient.

Yet the Psalms themselves reveal a far more complex picture of spiritual life. Many of the writers openly acknowledge that confusion, grief, and frustration are part of the human experience. Some psalms describe moments when the writer feels abandoned or overwhelmed by circumstances that seem impossible to understand. These expressions of distress are not presented as failures of faith. Instead, they show that honest struggle can coexist with trust in God — that the struggle and the trust are not opposites but companions.

This honesty reminds readers that faith is not a formula designed to remove every difficulty from life. It is a relationship that continues even when circumstances remain uncertain. The Psalms encourage people to bring their questions and concerns before God rather than suppressing them in the name of appearing faithful. The psalmists model something that many people find genuinely difficult: the willingness to tell God exactly what they are experiencing without softening it first.

Ignoring the Historical Context

A third misunderstanding occurs when readers overlook the historical setting in which the Psalms were written. Because the language of the poems can feel timeless, it is easy to forget that many of them emerged from specific moments in Israel's history — moments of military threat, political collapse, national exile, or hard-won restoration.

Some psalms reflect periods when the nation was secure and prosperous. Others arise from times of profound crisis. The writers occasionally refer to events such as the destruction of Jerusalem, the experience of living as captives in a foreign land, or the longing to return to a homeland that has been lost. Without recognizing these historical connections, readers may miss important layers of meaning within the poems.

Understanding the historical background does not diminish the relevance of the Psalms — it deepens it. When readers recognize that a psalm of lament was written by someone who had actually watched their city burn, or that a psalm of hope was composed by someone living in exile with no visible reason for optimism, the emotional weight of those poems becomes far more immediate. The prayers and songs preserved in the book are not abstract spiritual exercises. They are the responses of real people to real circumstances — and knowing something about those circumstances allows readers to receive them with appropriate gravity.

Treating the Psalms Only as Personal Devotion

Many readers approach the Psalms primarily as personal prayers designed for private reflection. While the book certainly contains language that individuals can use in their own spiritual practices, it was also deeply connected to the communal worship of Israel — and reading it only as private devotion misses a significant dimension of how it was written and why.

The Psalms were sung in the temple, recited during festivals, and shared among communities that gathered to remember their history and express their faith together. These settings shaped the way the psalms were written and preserved. Some poems invite entire groups to join in praise. Others reflect national concerns — the well-being of the king, the fate of Jerusalem, the identity of the people as a whole — that go far beyond the experience of any single individual.

When the Psalms are viewed only as private devotions, this broader dimension is easily overlooked. A reader who encounters a psalm expressing longing for the restoration of Jerusalem may struggle to connect with it personally if they do not recognize that it was written as a communal prayer — the voice of a whole people, not just one person. Understanding the communal dimension of the Psalms does not make them less personal. It adds a layer to their meaning: the individual voice and the community voice are both present in the same poem, and both are legitimate ways of inhabiting it.

Assuming Every Psalm Expresses the Same Emotion

Another common misunderstanding arises when readers assume that the Psalms should always convey the same emotional tone. Because many psalms celebrate joy and gratitude, some people expect the entire book to reflect a similar mood — and are surprised or unsettled when they encounter something darker.

In reality, the Psalms contain a wide range of emotional expression. Some poems are filled with praise and celebration, while others are marked by sorrow, anger, or confusion. These differences are not contradictions but reflections of the varied experiences that shape human life. The presence of lament alongside praise demonstrates that the writers did not feel compelled to hide their struggles. They brought every part of their experience into conversation with God, and the collection preserves that full range without apology.

Recognizing this emotional diversity prevents readers from forcing the Psalms into a single category — and from concluding, when they encounter a psalm that does not match their expectations, that something has gone wrong. A reader who expects the Psalms to be uniformly uplifting will find Psalm 88 deeply disorienting. A reader who understands that the collection was designed to hold the full range of human experience will recognize Psalm 88 as one of the collection's most honest and necessary poems. The difference between those two readings is entirely a matter of expectation.

Reading the Psalms Without Attention to Genre

A misunderstanding that often accompanies the others involves overlooking the literary nature of the book. The Psalms are written as poetry, and poetry communicates ideas in ways that differ from straightforward narrative or historical writing. When readers approach the Psalms expecting them to function like direct prose statements, they may misinterpret the imagery and language the poems employ.

Poetry frequently relies on metaphor, exaggeration, and symbolic language to express emotional or spiritual truths. When a psalm describes mountains skipping like rams or rivers clapping their hands, the writer is not attempting to describe literal events. The imagery communicates the overwhelming joy and celebration that accompany recognition of God's power and presence. Similarly, when a psalmist speaks about enemies surrounding them on every side or the earth trembling beneath God's voice, the language conveys the intensity of the experience rather than providing a technical description of events.

Recognizing the poetic nature of the Psalms also helps readers understand why the poems often move between different emotions within a few lines. Poetry allows writers to shift perspectives quickly, reflecting the changing thoughts and feelings that accompany real experiences. The psalmist may move from distress to hope, from gratitude to reflection, from complaint to confidence — not because the external situation has changed, but because the act of writing a poem is itself a process of working something out. Approaching the Psalms as poetry rather than as prose allows readers to follow that process rather than being confused by it.

Overlooking the Movement Within a Psalm

Closely related to the question of genre is the tendency to miss the internal movement that takes place within many individual psalms. Because the poems are often short, it can be tempting to read them quickly without noticing how the writer's perspective develops from beginning to end.

Yet many psalms follow a recognizable progression of thought. A lament psalm may begin with a cry for help, describing a situation that feels overwhelming or unjust. The writer then recalls past experiences of God's faithfulness, or reflects on the character of God as a source of stability. Gradually, the tone shifts — what began as a description of distress becomes a declaration of trust. The psalmist may conclude with praise or a promise to continue worshiping God once the situation changes.

This movement reveals the internal process through which the writer works through their emotions. The psalm is not a static expression of a single feeling. It captures a journey from one perspective to another — and the journey is the point. When readers focus only on a single line or phrase, they miss this dynamic process. The power of the psalm lies not only in its final words but in the path the writer takes to reach that conclusion. Reading the entire poem allows readers to witness a transformation that often mirrors their own experience of moving through difficulty toward something that resembles hope.

Ignoring the Diversity of Voices

Another misunderstanding arises when readers assume that the Psalms represent the perspective of a single author or voice. Because David is so frequently associated with the book, many people assume that he wrote every psalm — and read the collection accordingly, as the product of a single sensibility shaped by a single life.

In reality, the collection includes contributions from multiple writers across many generations. Some psalms are attributed to groups such as the sons of Korah, others to individuals like Asaph, Solomon, or Moses, and still others carry no attribution at all. Each of these contributors brought their own perspective, historical context, and spiritual experience to the collection.

Recognizing this diversity helps readers understand why the Psalms include such a wide range of perspectives without those perspectives needing to be harmonized into a single consistent voice. Some poems reflect the concerns of kings and leaders. Others express the experiences of ordinary individuals facing ordinary hardships. Certain psalms celebrate moments of national stability, while others arise from times of crisis and exile. Rather than presenting a single viewpoint, the Psalms capture the spiritual reflections of a community shaped by many different circumstances — and the breadth of that community is part of what makes the collection so durable.

Assuming Immediate Resolution

A further misunderstanding occurs when readers assume that every psalm will resolve its tension quickly and cleanly. Because some psalms end with confident statements of praise or trust, readers may expect every poem to follow the same arc — distress at the beginning, resolution by the end.

Yet not all psalms conclude with a clear resolution. Some poems end with questions that remain unanswered. The writer may continue to wrestle with confusion or distress without reaching a definitive conclusion. These endings reflect the reality that not every situation in life resolves neatly — and the Psalms, which were written to serve real communities facing real circumstances, do not pretend otherwise.

Rather than presenting unresolved endings as failures of faith, the Psalms preserve them as honest expressions of human experience. The writers continue to direct their words toward God even when clarity has not yet arrived. This willingness to remain in the tension of unanswered questions is itself a form of faithfulness — a refusal to manufacture a resolution that has not actually been reached. For readers who are living through seasons of unresolved difficulty, these psalms often provide more genuine companionship than the ones that conclude with praise.

Misunderstanding Expressions of Anger

Some readers are genuinely surprised — and sometimes troubled — by the intensity of emotion found in certain psalms. In a number of passages, the writers express anger toward enemies or call for justice in ways that feel uncomfortable by modern standards. These passages, sometimes called imprecatory psalms, ask God to act against those who have caused harm — often in vivid and unsparing language.

Without careful attention, these expressions are easily misunderstood. It is important to recognize that the Psalms are prayers spoken within the context of real situations involving conflict, injustice, and oppression. The writers are not describing abstract disagreements. They are responding to experiences that threatened their safety, their community, or their survival. The language reflects the intensity of those experiences honestly rather than softening them into something more palatable.

What is significant is where the anger is directed. Rather than acting on their rage, the psalmists bring it to God. They place the responsibility for justice within the hands of God rather than taking it into their own. This is not a minor distinction. It reflects a deep conviction that God is the final judge of human actions — and that the appropriate response to injustice is not private vengeance but honest prayer. By naming their anger before God rather than acting on it, the psalmists model a form of restraint that is also a form of trust.

For modern readers, these passages offer something important: permission to bring the full intensity of their emotional experience before God, including the parts that feel too raw or too ugly to express in polished religious language. The Psalms suggest that God can receive that honesty — and that offering it is better than suppressing it.

The Psalms as Formation

When these common misunderstandings are addressed, the purpose of the Psalms becomes considerably clearer. The book is not merely a source of comforting phrases or inspirational quotations. It is a carefully preserved anthology of prayers and songs that functions as a guide for shaping the spiritual life of those who engage with it seriously over time.

The variety of voices and emotions found within the Psalms invites readers to explore the complexity of their own experiences rather than simplifying them. Praise encourages gratitude. Lament provides language for confronting suffering. Reflections on justice challenge readers to consider how their actions affect others. The expressions of anger give permission for honesty. The unresolved endings teach patience. Through repeated reading and reflection, the Psalms gradually shape the way individuals think about faith, community, and the presence of God in everyday life — not by telling readers what to conclude, but by modeling a way of engaging with experience that is honest, persistent, and directed toward God.

This formative role helps explain why the Psalms have remained central to worship and spiritual practice across centuries and across such different cultures. Communities have returned to these poems again and again because they offer language that captures the full range of human experience — and because that language, repeated in worship and in private prayer, gradually becomes the reader's own.

Learning to Read the Psalms Thoughtfully

Approaching the Psalms thoughtfully involves a few simple but important habits. Reading each psalm as a complete poem — rather than stopping at a familiar verse — reveals how the writer's perspective develops from beginning to end. Considering the broader historical setting in which a psalm might have been written, even in general terms, adds depth to its meaning. Paying attention to the literary style — the repetition, the imagery, the parallel lines — reveals how the writer communicates ideas through poetic expression rather than direct statement. And reflecting on how the themes within a given psalm connect with the broader themes of the collection — praise, trust, lament, justice, kingship, and hope — creates a sense of continuity that enriches any individual poem.

None of this requires scholarly expertise. It requires only the willingness to slow down, to read a psalm more than once, and to ask what the whole poem is doing rather than what any single line can be made to mean. The Psalms reward that kind of attention generously. The reader who brings patience to the book will find that it gives back far more than the reader who comes only for a quick word of comfort — though it will often provide that too, precisely because the comfort it offers is grounded in something honest rather than something easy.

In the next chapter, we will explore how the themes and insights found within the Psalms continue to speak into modern life. Although the world in which the psalms were written differs from the present, the questions they address remain deeply relevant for readers today.

Chapter 7

What It Means for Modern Life

*"As the deer pants for streams of water, so my soul pants for you,
my God. My soul thirsts for God, for the living God. When can I
go and meet with God?"*
— Psalm 42:1–2

Ancient Words in a Modern World

When modern readers approach the book of Psalms, they often
encounter language and imagery that originated in a world very
different from their own. The psalmists wrote within the cultural
framework of ancient Israel, where daily life was shaped by
agriculture, temple worship, and the realities of political conflict
between neighboring kingdoms. References to shepherds, fortified
cities, sacrificial rituals, and royal authority reflect the historical
environment in which the poems were first composed.

At first glance, these elements may seem distant from modern
experience. Most readers today live in societies shaped by
technology, complex institutions, and rapid communication rather
than by the rhythms of ancient village life. Yet despite these
differences, the Psalms continue to function as practical resources
for people navigating the same pressures that human beings have
always faced.

The reason lies not in surface similarity but in a deeper one.
The external circumstances of life have changed dramatically over
time, yet the internal experiences that shape human existence have
remained remarkably consistent. People still wrestle with
uncertainty, search for meaning, express gratitude during
moments of joy, and seek comfort when confronted with grief or

injustice. The Psalms speak to those experiences not as historical artifacts but as living tools — available to anyone willing to use them.

This chapter examines what that use looks like in practice: how the Psalms change the way modern readers approach suffering, prayer, worship, community, and justice. Not what the Psalms meant in the ancient world — that has been the work of earlier chapters — but what they make possible today.

Finding Language for Difficult Moments

One of the most immediate and practical gifts the Psalms offer modern readers is language. There are moments in life when ordinary words fail — when grief cuts too deep, when fear has no clear object, when gratitude is so full it cannot be contained in normal speech. In those moments, people often fall silent not because they have nothing to say but because they cannot find the words for what they are carrying.

The Psalms step into that gap. They offer a vocabulary that reaches experiences that everyday language cannot easily access. The emotional intensity of grief, the quiet longing for reassurance, the stubborn persistence of hope in the face of discouraging circumstances — these are all given shape in the poems. Readers encountering the Psalms during difficult seasons often find that a line they have not thought about in years suddenly speaks with unexpected precision to what they are experiencing in the present moment.

This is not coincidence. The psalmists were writing from within real circumstances, and the poetry they produced carries the weight of those circumstances. When a modern reader picks up that weight — recognizes it as something they themselves are carrying — the distance of centuries collapses. The experience of finding language for what had been wordless is itself a form of relief. It means that what one is feeling has a name, that it has been felt before, that it belongs to something larger than the present moment of isolation.

This shared language matters especially during seasons when people feel most alone in their struggles. The Psalms remind readers that their experiences are part of a larger human story — that the terrain they are crossing has been crossed before, and that others have left words behind that can serve as markers for the path.

Honesty as a Spiritual Practice

Beyond providing language, the Psalms model something that many modern readers find genuinely countercultural: honesty as a form of spiritual practice. Contemporary culture frequently encourages people to manage the impression they make — to present composed, confident versions of themselves even when internal reality is considerably messier. This pressure shows up in social settings, professional environments, and often in religious communities as well, where there can be an unspoken expectation that faith should produce visible calm.

The Psalms offer a direct challenge to that expectation. The writers do not present polished versions of their spiritual lives. They describe loneliness, disappointment, confusion, and anger. They ask questions that have no immediate answer. They express frustration directly to God without first softening it into something more presentable. And the collection preserves these expressions without apology, treating them as legitimate and even necessary forms of spiritual engagement.

For modern readers, the practical implication is significant. The Psalms demonstrate that honesty before God is not a lapse in faith but an expression of it. A person does not need to have resolved their confusion before approaching God. They do not need to convert their grief into something more composed before it qualifies as prayer. The psalmists came with everything still unsettled, and the book treats that as the appropriate way to come

— not as a starting point to be moved past quickly, but as a valid and valued form of engagement with God.

Spiritual growth, the Psalms suggest, often begins precisely when people stop managing their inner lives and start naming them honestly. That naming is not weakness. It is where authentic faith begins.

Worship Beyond Celebration

The Psalms also challenge assumptions that many modern readers hold, often without realizing it, about the nature of worship. In many contemporary settings, worship is strongly associated with moments of celebration and gratitude — with music, gathering, and an emotional register that leans toward joy. The implicit message can be that if you are not feeling celebratory, you are perhaps not ready to worship, or that worship is what happens once the difficult season has passed.

The Psalms dismantle that assumption at every turn. Some of the most powerful psalms in the collection were written in moments when the writer's circumstances remained entirely unresolved — when the danger was still present, the illness was still progressing, the exile had not ended, and no visible sign of change was available. In those moments, the psalmists did not wait. They directed their words toward God anyway, not because the situation had improved but because the relationship persisted regardless of circumstances.

This is a practically important insight for modern readers. Worship, as the Psalms model it, is not a reward for favorable conditions. It is a posture — a sustained orientation toward God that continues through difficult seasons as well as easy ones. A person who can only worship when life is going well has a worship practice that will fail them at the moments when they most need it. The Psalms build a more durable practice: one that includes lament, confusion, and unresolved longing alongside praise and gratitude.

The lament psalms are not the B-side of the collection. They are among its most theologically serious contributions, demonstrating that turning toward God in the middle of pain is itself an act of faith — not a lesser form of worship but a form that takes the relationship seriously enough to bring the full truth of one's situation into it.

The Question of Suffering

One of the places where the Psalms speak most practically to modern readers is in how they handle suffering. Contemporary culture tends to treat suffering as a problem to be solved — a condition to be diagnosed, treated, or otherwise resolved as quickly as possible. The instinct is to move past pain rather than through it. Grief is allotted a timeline. Distress is expected to yield to intervention. People who remain in difficulty longer than expected are sometimes treated as though they are failing to recover rather than simply experiencing what grief and loss actually require.

The Psalms take a fundamentally different approach. The writers do not rush past suffering, and they do not explain it away. They sit inside it. Psalms of lament give extended attention to experiences of loss, injustice, illness, and abandonment, describing these realities in specific and sometimes striking terms without any attempt to soften or accelerate what is being experienced.

This willingness to remain present within suffering reflects an understanding of grief that many modern readers find both surprising and clarifying. The Psalms do not treat pain as something that must be overcome before meaningful spiritual life can continue. Instead, the experience of suffering becomes the very place where the writers seek God most urgently. The difficult season is not the interruption of faith. It is the context within which faith is most actively expressed.

For readers who have grown accustomed to the expectation that faith should produce comfort on a reasonable timeline, the lament psalms offer a different and more honest model. They demonstrate that sitting with difficult experiences — remaining present to them rather than rushing past them — is itself a legitimate and even necessary form of engagement with life and with God.

Justice as a Recurring Concern

The modern world is marked by persistent questions about fairness and justice. Whether in public conversations about inequality, personal experiences of mistreatment, or the broader sense that powerful forces operate beyond the reach of accountability, the concern for justice runs deeply through contemporary life. People want wrongs acknowledged, perpetrators held responsible, and systems changed. When those things do not happen — or happen too slowly, or incompletely — the resulting frustration can shade into despair or harden into cynicism.

The Psalms share this concern in ways that remain striking across the distance of centuries. Several psalms wrestle openly with the apparent success of those who act unjustly, observing the world as it actually is rather than as it should be. The writers do not pretend that wrongdoing always receives consequences or that righteous behavior guarantees protection from harm. They look at the actual state of affairs and bring their frustration forward honestly.

What distinguishes the psalmists' response, however, is where that frustration is directed. Rather than turning toward despair or retaliation, they bring their concerns before God. They appeal to a standard of justice that they believe stands above human institutions and human failure. This appeal does not resolve the injustice they see — the poems are honest enough not to pretend otherwise — but it places that injustice within a framework larger than the immediate moment. It refuses both resignation and cynicism by insisting that justice matters and that the appropriate response is continued appeal rather than abandonment of the concern.

For modern readers grappling with the same tensions, the Psalms offer a practical model for how those concerns can be held and expressed without collapsing under their weight. The writers maintain their conviction that justice matters even when its arrival remains uncertain — and they demonstrate that bringing that conviction before God, honestly and repeatedly, is itself a meaningful form of faithfulness.

Community and Shared Experience

Another practical dimension the Psalms offer modern readers involves the value of shared experience. In ancient Israel, the Psalms were not primarily private texts. They were sung and recited within communal settings — gatherings where individuals expressed their faith alongside others who were navigating similar struggles and hopes. The communal use of the Psalms meant that one person's lament could become the whole community's prayer, and one person's praise could become a shared declaration.

Modern societies often emphasize individual achievement and personal independence in ways that can produce significant isolation — including spiritual isolation. People navigate grief alone, process uncertainty alone, and sometimes carry burdens that were never meant to be carried by a single person without the presence of others. The communal dimension of the Psalms pushes back against that tendency.

Reading or praying the Psalms within a community changes how they function. Words that feel almost too honest to say alone become sayable when they are spoken together. A lament that might feel like an admission of weakness in private becomes an expression of shared humanity in community. The Psalms were designed to be used this way — to gather individual experience into a shared space where no one has to pretend that their difficulty is exceptional or their faith is more stable than it actually is.

For modern readers, this dimension of the Psalms is a reminder that spiritual reflection does not need to occur in isolation. Sharing the language of the Psalms within a community — whether in formal worship or in smaller, informal settings — provides encouragement and perspective that individuals often struggle to find on their own.

Reading the Psalms as a Unified Whole

One practical shift that significantly changes how readers benefit from the Psalms is approaching the book as a unified collection rather than a reservoir of individual verses to be extracted as needed. The tendency to pull a single line out of context — to treat the Psalms primarily as a source of quotable comfort — limits what the book can offer.

When the Psalms are read as a whole, patterns become visible that are invisible at the level of individual passages. The movement from lament toward praise across the five-book structure tells a story about how faith is tested and sustained over time. The placement of Psalm 1 at the beginning frames the entire collection as a reflection on wisdom and the life well-lived. The explosion of praise in the final psalms does not erase what came before but stands alongside it, showing that confidence and struggle are both part of a single ongoing relationship with God.

Modern readers who take time to read through the Psalms in sequence often discover dimensions of the book that surprise them. Voices they had not previously noticed come into focus. Themes that seemed disconnected reveal their relationship to one another. The collection becomes something richer than the sum of its individual parts — not a collection of isolated encouragements, but a sustained conversation about what it means to maintain faith through the full range of human experience.

The practical reward of this kind of reading is a more complete and more honest engagement with the book — and through the book, with the questions it has always been asking. The Psalms were not written to be encountered in fragments. They were written to be lived with, returned to, and discovered again across the changing seasons of a life.

A Living Tradition

The continued influence of the Psalms across centuries demonstrates that these writings have become part of a living tradition — one that has never stopped being used and never stopped finding new readers who recognize themselves within it. Communities of faith have returned to these poems in moments of celebration, mourning, and reflection, discovering new dimensions within familiar words as their own circumstances changed.

This ongoing engagement is itself a practical argument for the Psalms. They have been tested across an enormous range of human circumstances — political stability and exile, personal peace and individual crisis, funerals and festivals, elaborate temple ceremonies and solitary prayer in quiet rooms. The same texts have continued to serve all of these situations because they were built for exactly this kind of range. They were never written to speak to only one kind of moment.

As individuals encounter the Psalms today, they join a long line of readers who have turned to these writings for guidance, comfort, and perspective — and found that the book had something to offer that matched what they were actually carrying. That track record is not incidental. It is part of what the Psalms are.

Chapter 8

Modern Reflection

"Search me, God, and know my heart; test me and know my
anxious thoughts. See if there is any offensive way in me, and lead
me in the way everlasting."
— Psalm 139:23–24

What the Psalms Do to the Reader

The previous chapter examined what modern readers can do with
the Psalms — how they can be used as practical resources for
navigating suffering, prayer, worship, and community. This
chapter is concerned with a different question: what the Psalms do
to the reader. Not the immediate application of a text but the
slower, less visible work that happens when a person engages with
the Psalms seriously and repeatedly over time.

The distinction matters because the Psalms were never only
about providing tools for specific situations. They were designed
to form people — to shape the habits of mind and heart through
which individuals interpret their experiences and orient themselves
toward God. That kind of formation does not happen in a single
reading. It accumulates across years of return, across different
seasons of life, across the gradual process of allowing a particular
kind of language and reflection to become one's own.

The opening verse of the Psalter sets this expectation from
the start. The person described as blessed in Psalm 1 is not
someone who has consulted the book in a moment of crisis. It is
someone who meditates on it day and night — who has made
sustained attention to this kind of reflection a defining practice of

their life. That is the posture the Psalms are ultimately designed to cultivate, and it is the posture this chapter explores.

The Rhythm of Human Experience

Formation through the Psalms begins with recognition. The collection does not follow a straight emotional line — it cycles, shifts, returns to familiar places from new angles, and refuses to settle into a single sustained mood. This is not a structural weakness. It is an accurate representation of what human experience actually looks like across time.

Life moves in cycles. Periods of stability are interrupted by disruption. Clarity gives way to confusion. Confidence is tested by uncertainty and sometimes dismantled entirely, only to be rebuilt on different ground. The Psalms preserve this rhythm within their arrangement — psalms of confident praise sit beside psalms of unresolved lament, and neither is presented as the definitive emotional state toward which the others are moving. Both are authentic. Both belong.

Readers who stay with the Psalms over time begin to internalize this rhythm. They learn that their own emotional and spiritual cycles are not signs of instability or failure but reflections of how life actually unfolds. A person who has prayed through the Psalms in a season of confidence and then returned to them in a season of crisis discovers something important: the book has always been here. The language was always there for both. Neither season disqualifies the other, and neither is more spiritually legitimate than the one that preceded it.

What is notable is how rarely the psalmists treat their emotional shifts as something to be corrected or concealed. A writer may move from despair to praise within a single poem, and neither state is framed as a failure. Both are treated as honest responses to real conditions. Over time, that modeling gives readers permission to allow their own inner lives to move and shift without demanding that the movement conform to a prescribed pattern. Formation through the Psalms is partly the slow acquisition of that permission — learning to inhabit one's actual experience rather than the experience one feels one ought to be having.

Attention and the Reshaping of Perception

The deeper challenge of modern life is not simply that it moves too fast, though it does. The deeper challenge is that the pace of modern life shapes how people think — training them to respond quickly, move on rapidly, and treat depth as a luxury rather than a necessity. The habits of attention that digital culture reinforces are habits of surface engagement: scan, react, continue. Applied to one's inner life, those habits produce people who are very busy experiencing things and very poorly equipped to understand what they are experiencing.

The Psalms interrupt this pattern. They do not merely ask readers to pause — they model a different relationship to experience altogether. The writers return to the same events, the same questions, and the same themes from multiple angles across many poems. They do not extract a lesson from an experience and move on. They circle back, look again, ask the question differently, sit with what does not resolve. The repetition across 150 poems is not redundancy. It is the practice of sustained attention applied to the things that matter most — the kind of attention that eventually produces understanding rather than merely accumulating impressions.

Readers who engage with the Psalms regularly over time often find that this practice begins to transfer. The habit of returning to something, examining it from a different angle, refusing to let it remain unexamined — this becomes a way of processing one's own experience. Not because readers are consciously imitating the psalmists, but because the sustained encounter with that kind of reflection gradually reshapes how reflection happens.

This is the distinction between information and formation. Information tells readers something. Formation changes how they see. The Psalms are not primarily informational — they do not communicate a set of facts to be retained and applied. They are formative — they model a way of inhabiting experience that, over time, becomes the reader's own way of inhabiting it. That is what Psalm 1 is pointing toward when it describes the blessed person as one who meditates day and night: not someone who has read the Psalms, but someone who has been changed by sustained engagement with them.

Memory and Perspective

One of the practices the Psalms model most consistently — and one that shapes readers most durably over time — is the deliberate act of remembering. The writers regularly look back to earlier moments: times of provision, guidance, or restoration that came before the present difficulty. They do not use these memories as escapes from the present. They bring them into the present as evidence — as arguments for hope based on what has already occurred.

This practice works against one of the most reliable features of difficulty: its tendency to feel total. When circumstances are genuinely hard, the present moment has a way of expanding until it fills the entire frame. The difficulty becomes not merely what is happening now but the whole story, the defining reality, the ground truth against which everything else must be measured. Memory is the discipline that counters this. It introduces a longer view — it asks what else is also true, what has been navigated before, what evidence from earlier seasons might speak to this one.

Readers who stay with the Psalms over time absorb this practice. They learn it not by studying it abstractly but by encountering it repeatedly across the collection, in different voices and different circumstances, until it begins to feel like a natural response rather than a learned technique. When difficulty arrives, the habit of reaching back — of asking what has been true before, of finding in personal or communal history a reason to hold on — becomes available because it has been modeled so consistently.

The psalmists also practice this remembering in a communal dimension, drawing not only on personal experience but on the inherited memory of the community. A writer facing circumstances they have never personally navigated can still reach back to what an earlier generation experienced and find in that record a source of confidence. This communal memory carries a particular resonance for modern readers who feel cut off from inherited confidence — who sense that their personal history is too thin to carry much weight on its own. The Psalms invite them into a longer story. They do not need to carry the entire weight of evidence alone. Others have gone before, and their testimony still speaks.

Language for Prayer

The Psalms also perform a formative function in how prayer is understood and practiced. In many religious settings, prayer carries a set of implicit expectations — about the appropriate tone, the required composure, the kind of language that qualifies as genuine address to God. Those expectations are rarely stated directly, but they shape behavior. People arrive at prayer having already filtered their experience, presenting a version of themselves that feels appropriate rather than one that reflects what they are actually carrying.

The Psalms consistently subvert this filtering. The writers bring confusion into prayer without waiting for it to resolve. They bring anger without converting it into something more temperate. They bring grief in its rawest form, before it has been processed into anything more manageable. They ask why God seems absent without first constructing a theologically defensible framework for the question. The language is unmediated in ways that can feel startling to readers accustomed to more controlled forms of religious expression.

This unmediated quality is not a failure of the writers' composure. It is a deliberate feature of the prayer they are modeling — one that reflects a particular understanding of what prayer is for. Prayer in the Psalms is not performance. It is speech. It is the act of bringing what is real before the one who is real, without managing the encounter into something more comfortable. Formation through the Psalms involves gradually learning that this kind of directness is not only permitted but valued — that what is actually felt and thought is already sufficient material for prayer, and that bringing those realities forward, rather than managing them first, is itself a form of trust.

Over time, readers who inhabit the Psalms find that their own prayer begins to change. Not because they have adopted a new technique but because the repeated encounter with that kind of speech gradually expands what feels possible. The range of what can be brought before God widens. The threshold of what requires preparation before it can be offered lowers. The Psalms form readers into people who can pray more honestly — and that formation is one of the most practical gifts the book gives.

A Voice for the Human Heart

Beneath the specific practices the Psalms model — remembering, attending, praying honestly — there is something more fundamental that sustained engagement with the Psalms cultivates: a particular relationship to the deeper questions of life. Questions about meaning, justice, purpose, and direction do not disappear when life is going well. They go quiet, perhaps, or lose their urgency. But they resurface reliably in moments of pressure or transition, and when they do, they require some framework for holding them without being undone by them.

The Psalms build that framework over time. The writers do not avoid the hard questions or resolve them prematurely. They allow them to develop, to be asked from multiple angles, to remain open for the length of a poem or a book or a lifetime. Through poetry and reflection, they express a consistent desire for a world marked by justice, faithfulness, and restoration — while remaining clear-eyed about the distance between that world and the one they actually inhabit.

What the Psalms offer is not resolution so much as company. The writers have been in the same places — the places of waiting, of unanswered need, of grief that seems to have no bottom, of joy that arrives unexpectedly and does not stay as long as one had hoped. They have asked the same questions and not always received clear answers. Yet they have continued. That continuation is itself part of what the Psalms communicate. To keep speaking, to keep returning, to keep bringing life before God even when the response is not yet visible — that is the posture the book models from beginning to end. Formation through the Psalms is, in the end, the slow acquisition of that posture.

Continuing the Conversation

To read the Psalms seriously is to step into something already in motion. These writings have been carried across centuries, spoken and repeated in settings of grief, gratitude, and reflection. They have shaped how individuals and communities understand both life and faith — not by telling people what to conclude but by demonstrating, again and again, what it looks like to bring experience honestly into relationship with God.

There is something worth pausing on in the sheer breadth of that continuity. These poems have been read in circumstances as varied as human history itself — in periods of political stability and in the middle of exile, in moments of personal peace and in the depths of individual crisis. They have been sung in elaborate temple ceremonies and whispered alone in quiet rooms. They have accompanied funerals and festivals, national mourning and national celebration. The fact that the same texts have continued to serve such an enormous range of human situations is not incidental. It points to something in the Psalms that operates at a level deeper than any single circumstance — a quality that transcends the specific and speaks to the enduring.

For the modern reader, this means that engaging seriously with the Psalms is not an exercise in recovering something that once mattered but no longer does. It is an encounter with a living body of reflection that has never stopped being used, never stopped being returned to, never stopped finding new readers who recognize themselves within it. The conversation the psalmists began has not concluded. Each person who reads these poems with genuine attention becomes part of that ongoing exchange — not as a passive recipient, but as someone whose own experience now enters into dialogue with the voices the book preserves.

The invitation is not simply to understand the Psalms from the outside. It is to allow them to do what they have always done — to meet readers where they actually are, to give shape to what they are carrying, and to draw that experience into the larger conversation about what it means to live, to believe, and to continue seeking in the middle of a world that does not always make those things easy. That is what the Psalms have always been for. And that is what they remain.

Chapter 9

Reflection Questions

"I will consider all your works and meditate on all your mighty deeds. Your ways, God, are holy. What God is as great as our God?"
— Psalm 77:12–13

The Psalms invite readers into a conversation that has unfolded across centuries. Rather than presenting a rigid system of ideas, the book offers a collection of voices that wrestle with life's complexities while continuing to seek God. Each psalm captures a moment of reflection shaped by real experience — moments of gratitude, distress, uncertainty, and hope.

Because of this, engaging with the Psalms often raises questions that lead readers into deeper reflection. The writers do not attempt to resolve every tension they encounter. Instead, they speak honestly about their experiences and bring their thoughts before God. Their words invite readers to participate in the same process.

For many people, the Psalms become most meaningful when they are approached not simply as ancient poetry but as a conversation that continues into the present. The emotions expressed in the book — joy, sorrow, trust, confusion, gratitude, and longing — remain part of human experience today. This continuity is not accidental. It reflects the fact that the questions the psalmists carried are the same questions that surface in every generation, regardless of how different the surrounding world may look.

The following questions are designed to help readers reflect on how the themes of the Psalms connect with their own lives.

Some focus on the emotional honesty found throughout the book, while others explore broader ideas related to faith, suffering, community, and hope. They are not intended to produce simple answers. Instead, they encourage thoughtful engagement with the text and invite readers to consider how the insights of the Psalms might influence their understanding of life and faith.

These questions can be approached individually or discussed within a group setting. Either approach allows space for the ideas found within the Psalms to take root through careful consideration. There is value in both — private reflection tends to surface personal connections that might not emerge in conversation, while group discussion often introduces perspectives that an individual reader would not have reached alone. The Psalms themselves model both modes: some were composed as personal prayers, others as communal songs. Both have their place.

When readers pause to consider the themes within these poems, they often begin to recognize how the experiences of the psalmists connect with their own. That recognition is frequently where the most meaningful engagement begins.

1. The Role of Emotion in Faith

One of the most striking features of the Psalms is the wide range of emotions expressed throughout the book. The writers do not limit themselves to calm expressions of praise or carefully structured prayers. Instead, they speak openly about joy, sorrow, gratitude, frustration, anger, and uncertainty. Some psalms celebrate moments of deliverance and renewal. Others describe seasons when the writer feels abandoned or overwhelmed. These contrasting emotions appear side by side within the same collection, which itself communicates something important: the book does not ask readers to leave their emotional reality at the door in order to engage with it.

This emotional honesty reveals that faith in the Psalms is not portrayed as a steady, undisturbed state. Instead, it reflects the full complexity of human life — faith as it is actually lived rather than as it is sometimes idealized.

Reflect on the following questions:

- How does the emotional openness of the Psalms compare with the way faith is often discussed in modern culture?
- Do contemporary conversations about faith sometimes emphasize confidence and certainty while overlooking the role of struggle and doubt?
- Why do you think the writers of the Psalms were willing to express such strong emotions in their prayers?
- What might these expressions suggest about the relationship between honesty and faith?
- How might the Psalms encourage people to approach prayer or reflection with greater openness about their experiences?
- In what ways could acknowledging difficult emotions strengthen rather than weaken spiritual growth?

The Psalms demonstrate that emotional honesty can coexist with trust in God. Rather than presenting faith as a posture that conceals uncertainty, the book portrays it as a relationship that allows space for genuine expression. The psalmists show that faith does not eliminate the reality of human emotion but provides a context in which those emotions can be named, brought forward, and held within a larger frame of meaning. That willingness to speak honestly — without first having everything sorted — is itself an act of trust, and the Psalms treat it as such throughout.

2. Responding to Uncertainty

Many psalms were written during periods when the writer faced circumstances that felt confusing or overwhelming. These situations might involve danger from enemies, illness, injustice, or uncertainty about the future. Rather than ignoring these realities, the psalmists describe them openly. They ask questions about why hardship occurs and seek reassurance that God remains attentive to their concerns. At the same time, many of these poems move gradually toward expressions of trust or hope — not because the circumstances have changed, but because the act of bringing them honestly before God has shifted something in the writer's perspective.

Consider the following questions:

- What do the Psalms suggest about how individuals can respond when life feels uncertain or unstable?
- How do the writers balance honest questions with statements of trust in God?
- Why might this balance be important when navigating difficult situations?
- How do the psalmists continue their conversation with God even when answers do not immediately appear?
- What might modern readers learn from the way the psalmists bring their uncertainties into prayer?

The Psalms demonstrate that faith does not require perfect clarity before it can be expressed. Instead, it involves continuing the search for understanding even when circumstances remain unresolved. That willingness to remain engaged — to keep speaking, to keep returning — is itself a form of trust. For modern readers conditioned to expect relatively quick resolution, the lament psalms in particular offer a different rhythm: one in which waiting is not a failure of faith but a legitimate and even necessary part of its development.

3. The Importance of Memory

Memory plays an important role throughout the Psalms. Many writers recall earlier events in which they believe God acted on behalf of the people or provided guidance during difficult times. These memories serve as reminders that present challenges are not the entire story. By reflecting on the past, the psalmists strengthen their confidence that restoration and renewal may still be possible — that what has been true before can be true again.

This use of memory is worth examining carefully, because it is not simply a matter of looking backward. The psalmists use the past as an active resource for the present. They reach into what has already been experienced — collectively or individually — and draw from it something that helps them hold steady in the current moment.

Consider the following questions:

- Why do you think remembering past experiences plays such an important role in sustaining hope?
- How might reflecting on personal history help individuals respond more thoughtfully to present challenges?
- In what ways do communities benefit from remembering events that shaped their identity?
- How do stories passed down through generations influence the way people understand their lives today?
- What examples from your own life illustrate the importance of remembering moments of resilience or guidance?

The Psalms suggest that memory is not simply a way of looking backward. It becomes a tool for navigating the present. By recalling earlier moments of help or restoration, individuals gain perspective that can strengthen their ability to face new challenges. Communities that maintain a shared memory of how they have come through difficulty before are better equipped to face new difficulty with something more than anxiety — they carry with them evidence that hard seasons are not necessarily permanent.

4. Individual Faith and Community

Although many psalms sound deeply personal, they were often shared within communal settings. Worship gatherings in ancient Israel included music, singing, and spoken responses that allowed entire communities to participate in prayer and reflection. These shared experiences reinforced a sense of collective identity. When individuals expressed their concerns or gratitude through the language of the Psalms, others could recognize their own experiences within those words — and in that recognition, something important happened. The individual's experience was validated, and the community was reminded of its shared humanity before God.

This dynamic is not simply a historical curiosity. It points to something that remains true about how faith develops: it tends to deepen within relationships, not only in solitude.

Consider these questions:

- Why might it have been important for these prayers and songs to be shared within a community rather than kept private?
- How does communal worship influence the way individuals experience faith?
- In what ways can shared reflection strengthen resilience during difficult seasons?
- Why do people often feel encouraged when they discover that others share similar struggles?
- How might modern communities create opportunities for meaningful shared reflection?

The communal nature of the Psalms reminds readers that faith is not solely an individual journey. It often develops within relationships that provide encouragement, accountability, and perspective. The isolation that characterizes much of modern life — including, at times, modern religious life — runs against the grain of what the Psalms model. They were written to be shared, to be spoken in the presence of others, to be returned to again and again within a community that could carry the words together even when individuals found them difficult to carry alone.

5. Language for the Human Experience

Many people struggle to find words that adequately describe their emotions during moments of intense experience. Grief, joy, uncertainty, and gratitude can feel difficult to express in ordinary language. The Psalms offer a vocabulary for these experiences through poetry and imagery — a vocabulary that has proven remarkably durable across very different cultures and historical periods.

Part of what makes this vocabulary so effective is that it does not try to be precise in the way that analytical language is precise. Instead, it reaches for images and comparisons that allow readers to feel their way into meaning rather than think their way toward it. A shepherd and a flock, a fortress in a storm, a deer seeking water — these images communicate something that a definition cannot.

Consider the following questions:

- Have you ever encountered a psalm that seemed to describe an experience you found difficult to articulate?
- Why do you think poetry and music are often powerful ways of expressing spiritual reflection?
- What role does imagery play in helping readers connect emotionally with the text?
- How does the poetic style of the Psalms influence the way readers interpret their meaning?
- In what ways can language shape the way individuals understand their experiences?

The Psalms demonstrate that poetry can provide a bridge between emotion and reflection. Through imagery and metaphor, the writers create space for readers to recognize their own experiences within the text. That recognition is often the beginning of something larger — not just the sense of being understood, but the sense of being invited into a framework within which those experiences can be further explored and interpreted.

6. Faith in a Changing World

The world in which the Psalms were written differs significantly from modern society. Ancient Israel was shaped by agricultural rhythms, temple worship, and regional political conflict. Modern life, by contrast, includes rapid communication, global interconnectedness, and complex social systems that the psalmists could not have imagined. Despite these differences, the Psalms continue to resonate with readers across cultures — which raises an interesting question about what exactly is carrying across that distance.

The answer seems to lie not in the surface details of the world the psalmists inhabited, but in the underlying structure of the questions they were asking. Those questions — about justice, about suffering, about the reliability of God, about what it means to live well in an uncertain world — have not become obsolete. They have simply taken on new forms in new circumstances.

Consider these questions:

- What themes within the Psalms seem most relevant to modern life?

- How do the emotional experiences described in the Psalms remain recognizable today?

- What challenges do modern readers face when interpreting ancient texts?

- How can understanding the historical context of the Psalms enhance their meaning?

- In what ways might ancient wisdom offer perspective for navigating contemporary challenges?

The enduring influence of the Psalms suggests that certain human concerns remain consistent across generations. The external world may change dramatically, but the search for meaning, justice, and hope continues. Readers who take the time to understand the historical distance between themselves and the psalmists often find, perhaps unexpectedly, that crossing that distance brings them closer to something in the text — and in themselves — that they had not previously recognized.

7. The Search for Meaning

Throughout the Psalms, writers wrestle with profound questions about life. They ask why injustice sometimes appears to prevail, why suffering occurs, and how individuals can maintain hope during difficult circumstances. These questions are not unique to the ancient world. Across cultures and generations, people continue to reflect on similar concerns — and continue to find that the Psalms speak to them with unexpected directness.

What is notable about how the psalmists approach these questions is that they do not treat them as problems to be solved before faith can proceed. The questions and the faith exist together, in the same poems, spoken by the same voices. The search for meaning is not positioned as an obstacle to belief but as an expression of it.

Consider the following questions:

- Why do questions about justice, suffering, and purpose continue to appear across different cultures and historical periods?
- What insights do the Psalms offer for individuals who are searching for meaning in their own lives?
- How do the writers approach questions that do not have simple answers?
- Why might reflection and prayer be important tools for exploring life's deeper questions?

- In what ways can engaging with ancient texts broaden a person's understanding of faith and purpose?

The Psalms demonstrate that the search for meaning is a central part of human life — not a detour from faith but a dimension of it. Rather than avoiding difficult questions, the writers bring them into their conversations with God. Their example encourages readers to approach life with curiosity and honesty, trusting that the act of asking, even without receiving an immediate answer, is itself a meaningful form of engagement.

Continuing the Reflection

These questions represent only a starting point for engaging with the themes found in the Psalms. Each reader will encounter the book from a unique perspective shaped by personal experience, cultural background, and spiritual history. What surfaces for one reader may not surface for another, and that diversity of response is not a problem to be resolved but a reflection of the breadth of the book itself.

As individuals reflect on the Psalms, new insights often emerge over time. A passage that once seemed distant may later feel deeply relevant during a particular season of life. Questions that once seemed answerable may reopen. Questions that once felt urgent may settle into something quieter and more sustainable. The Psalms accommodate all of these movements because they were never intended to be encountered once and set aside.

In this way, the Psalms continue to function as living texts that speak across generations. By returning to these poems again and again, readers participate in a conversation that has unfolded for thousands of years — a conversation that invites each generation to explore the enduring questions of faith, suffering, gratitude, and hope, and to bring their own experience into that ongoing exchange.

Chapter 10

Five Lessons

*"The Lord is compassionate and gracious, slow to anger, abounding
in love. He will not always accuse, nor will he harbor his anger
forever."*
— Psalm 103:8–9

The book of Psalms contains a remarkable collection of
reflections shaped by the experiences of individuals and
communities across many generations. These poems were written
in different historical periods and emerged from a variety of
circumstances, yet they share common concerns that continue to
resonate with readers today. Some psalms arise from moments of
celebration and gratitude, while others emerge from seasons of
hardship, confusion, or longing.

Despite this diversity, several themes appear repeatedly
throughout the collection. When these themes are examined
together, they reveal enduring insights about the nature of faith,
the realities of human experience, and the ways individuals seek
meaning within their lives.

The lessons that emerge from the Psalms are not presented as
rigid rules or abstract theories. Instead, they appear through the
lived reflections of people who sought to understand their
experiences in relationship with God. Their words provide
guidance not by eliminating life's complexity, but by
demonstrating how faith can engage honestly with that
complexity.

The following five lessons highlight some of the most
important insights that arise from the Psalms. While each reader
may discover additional themes within the book, these lessons

provide a helpful framework for understanding why the Psalms have remained meaningful across centuries.

1. Faith Includes Honest Expression

One of the most striking features of the Psalms is the honesty with which the writers describe their experiences. Rather than presenting faith as a constant state of confidence or certainty, the psalmists openly acknowledge moments of confusion, frustration, grief, and longing. Their prayers do not attempt to conceal difficult emotions or replace them with artificial optimism.

Instead, the writers bring the full range of their experiences into conversation with God. They describe fear when danger approaches, sorrow when loss occurs, and frustration when injustice appears to prevail. In doing so, they reveal that faith is not built upon the denial of hardship but upon the willingness to confront life honestly.

This openness challenges the assumption that spiritual life must always appear composed or unwavering. In many modern settings, individuals may feel pressure to present themselves as confident in their beliefs even when they are wrestling with uncertainty. The Psalms offer a different perspective. They demonstrate that authentic faith can include questions, doubts, and moments of emotional struggle.

By speaking openly about their circumstances, the psalmists show that honesty is not a sign of weak faith. Instead, it becomes an essential part of a genuine relationship with God. Their words suggest that spiritual growth often begins when individuals acknowledge their experiences without attempting to disguise them.

This lesson remains relevant for readers today. Many people encounter seasons in which their lives do not unfold according to their expectations. During such moments, it can be tempting to withdraw from spiritual reflection or to suppress difficult emotions. The Psalms remind readers that these struggles can become part of the conversation with God rather than obstacles that prevent it.

The honesty found throughout the Psalms ultimately reveals a deeper understanding of faith. Rather than requiring perfect emotional stability, faith invites individuals to bring every part of their lives — joy, sorrow, hope, and uncertainty — into a relationship with God. The psalmists did not wait until their circumstances improved before speaking. They spoke from within the difficulty, and the act of speaking was itself an expression of trust.

It is also worth noting that the Psalms do not treat honesty as a single moment of breakthrough. The same writers who lament in one psalm appear to praise in another, and then lament again. The pattern repeats because that is how human experience actually moves — not in a straight line toward resolution, but in cycles that return to familiar struggles from new vantage points. The Psalms normalize that pattern rather than treating it as a problem to be overcome.

2. Worship Extends Beyond Celebration

Another important lesson found within the Psalms involves the nature of worship. Many people associate worship primarily with moments of joy or gratitude. Celebrations, songs of praise, and expressions of thanksgiving often come to mind when the word worship is mentioned.

The Psalms certainly contain many examples of these joyful expressions. Numerous poems celebrate God's greatness, acknowledge His provision, and invite communities to respond with praise. Yet the book also includes many psalms written during periods of hardship, confusion, or distress.

Some writers describe situations in which they feel surrounded by enemies or overwhelmed by circumstances beyond their control. Others speak from the depths of grief or disappointment. Even in these moments, however, the psalmists continue to direct their words toward God.

This pattern suggests that worship is not limited to favorable circumstances. Instead, it becomes a way of maintaining perspective during seasons when life feels uncertain. By turning toward God even in the midst of hardship, the psalmists demonstrate that worship can include both praise and lament.

This broader understanding of worship challenges the idea that spiritual devotion must always be joyful or triumphant. The Psalms show that expressions of sorrow, questioning, and longing can also be forms of worship when they are brought honestly before God.

For modern readers, this insight can reshape the way spiritual practices are understood. Worship does not need to wait until problems are resolved or circumstances improve. Instead, it can occur during the very moments when life feels most uncertain.

In this way, the Psalms encourage individuals to maintain their connection with God regardless of the conditions they face. Worship becomes not merely a response to blessings but also a source of strength and perspective during difficult seasons.

What the lament psalms demonstrate, specifically, is that turning toward God in the middle of pain is itself a meaningful act — not a lesser form of worship that must eventually graduate into praise, but a legitimate expression of faith in its own right. Some of the most theologically rich psalms in the entire collection are psalms of lament. They do not resolve quickly. They sit in the difficulty, and the act of remaining there while still addressing God is what gives them their particular power. Readers who have experienced prolonged hardship often find these psalms more sustaining than psalms of praise, precisely because they do not require the reader to feel something they do not currently feel.

3. Remembering Shapes Perspective

A third lesson that appears repeatedly throughout the Psalms involves the importance of memory. The writers frequently recall earlier moments when they believe God acted on behalf of the people. These memories often include stories of deliverance, protection, or guidance during difficult periods in Israel's history.

By recalling these events, the psalmists remind themselves that present challenges do not represent the entire story. Even when current circumstances appear discouraging, memories of past restoration provide reasons to hope for renewal.

This emphasis on remembering plays a powerful role within the spiritual life of the community. The Psalms encourage individuals to look beyond their immediate experiences and consider the broader narrative that has shaped their lives.

For modern readers, this lesson highlights the importance of perspective. When individuals focus solely on present difficulties, those challenges can appear overwhelming. Yet reflecting on earlier moments of resilience or unexpected help can offer reassurance that difficult seasons are not permanent.

Memory also plays an important role within communities. Shared stories of hardship and restoration often become part of a group's collective identity. These stories remind future generations that previous challenges were faced and overcome.

The Psalms demonstrate how remembering can strengthen faith by placing current experiences within a larger framework. By recalling the past, the writers gain confidence that their present circumstances may eventually give way to new possibilities.

This practice encourages readers today to reflect thoughtfully on their own histories. Moments of guidance, perseverance, and renewal may provide insight that helps navigate the challenges of the present.

There is a discipline involved in this kind of remembering that is easily underestimated. In moments of acute difficulty, the natural tendency is to narrow focus — to see only what is immediately in front of us, to feel only what is most pressing. Memory pushes back against that narrowing. It requires the deliberate choice to widen the frame, to ask what else is also true, to reach back into personal or communal history for evidence that the present moment is not the whole story. The psalmists practice this discipline not occasionally but consistently, and the Psalms preserve that practice as a model for their readers.

4. Faith Is Both Personal and Communal

The Psalms reveal another important dimension of spiritual life: faith involves both personal reflection and communal experience. Many psalms express deeply personal emotions, describing the inner thoughts and struggles of the writer. These reflections give readers a glimpse into the individual experiences that shaped the poems.

At the same time, the Psalms were often used within communal worship settings. They were sung during gatherings at the temple, recited during festivals, and shared among communities seeking to express their faith together.

This combination of personal reflection and communal participation highlights the dual nature of spiritual life. Individuals bring their own experiences into their relationship with God, yet they also find strength through connection with others who share similar hopes and questions.

Communities provide opportunities for encouragement and shared understanding. When individuals gather to reflect on their experiences together, they discover that many of their struggles and hopes are not unique. Others have faced similar circumstances and have sought meaning in similar ways.

The communal dimension of the Psalms also reinforces the idea that faith is shaped not only by private reflection but also by shared practices. Singing, prayer, and collective remembrance help create a sense of belonging that strengthens the spiritual life of the community.

For modern readers, this lesson emphasizes the importance of relationships in the development of faith. While personal reflection remains valuable, spiritual growth often occurs more deeply when individuals engage with others who share their journey.

One consequence of the communal use of the Psalms is that an individual's experience becomes connected to something larger than itself. When a person in private distress brings a lament psalm into a gathered community, that distress is no longer entirely private. It is recognized, held, and shared. The community does not necessarily resolve the problem, but it changes the nature of how the problem is carried. This is part of what the Psalms were designed to do — not to remove difficulty from individual experience, but to ensure that no one carried it entirely alone.

5. The Search for Meaning Continues

Perhaps the most enduring lesson found within the Psalms is that the search for meaning remains a central part of human life. Throughout the book, the writers wrestle with questions about justice, suffering, purpose, and hope. These questions arise repeatedly as the psalmists attempt to understand the events unfolding around them.

At times, they express confidence that God's justice will prevail. At other moments, they struggle to reconcile their expectations with the realities they observe. Their reflections reveal that faith does not eliminate the need for thoughtful questioning.

Instead, the Psalms portray a process of reflection that unfolds gradually. The writers bring their questions before God, trusting that their concerns are heard even when answers remain unclear.

This willingness to engage with life's deeper questions allows the Psalms to remain relevant across generations. Every era encounters circumstances that raise similar concerns about fairness, suffering, and the meaning of human existence.

The psalmists do not claim to possess simple solutions to these questions. Rather than offering a final explanation for every difficulty, they demonstrate how faith can continue even when understanding is incomplete.

For readers today, this lesson offers encouragement to approach life with openness and curiosity. The search for meaning does not need to be avoided or rushed toward easy conclusions. Instead, it can become a thoughtful journey shaped by reflection, prayer, and trust.

The Psalms remind readers that engaging with these questions is itself part of spiritual growth. By continuing to seek understanding, individuals participate in the same conversation that has unfolded across centuries.

What is perhaps most striking about this lesson is the absence of resolution in so many of the psalms that raise the hardest questions. The book does not conclude with a theological explanation for why suffering occurs or why injustice persists. It concludes with praise — but that praise comes after 149 preceding poems, many of which remain unresolved. The movement toward praise at the end of the Psalter is not a retraction of the laments that came before. It is a decision, made in full awareness of everything that has already been expressed, to affirm that God is still worthy of worship. That is a very different kind of confidence than one that has never been tested, and it is the kind the Psalms consistently model.

The Enduring Wisdom of the Psalms

Taken together, these five lessons reveal why the Psalms continue to speak to readers today. The book captures the complexity of human experience while pointing toward a relationship with God that remains present through every season of life.

The psalmists demonstrate that faith can include honesty, questioning, remembrance, community, and the ongoing search for meaning. Their reflections invite readers to approach their own experiences with the same openness and willingness to engage deeply with life's challenges. What the five lessons share is a common resistance to simplification. None of them offer a formula. None of them promise that applying the right approach will produce a predictable result. Instead, they describe a way of inhabiting life — with greater honesty, wider perspective, deeper connection, and more patient curiosity — that the psalmists found sustainable across many different kinds of circumstances.

In doing so, the Psalms continue to offer guidance not through rigid answers but through a model of thoughtful reflection that remains relevant in every generation.

Continuing the Conversation

One of the most remarkable aspects of the Psalms is the way they continue to invite participation from each new generation of readers. The writers who composed these poems could not have imagined the countless individuals who would later encounter their words across different cultures and centuries. Yet the questions they raised and the reflections they shared remain recognizable today.

When readers engage with the Psalms, they enter into a conversation that stretches across history. They encounter voices that speak from another era yet still address concerns that remain deeply familiar. This conversation allows readers to explore their own experiences through the wisdom preserved within the text.

The Psalms do not demand that readers adopt a particular interpretation or reach immediate conclusions. Instead, they create space for thoughtful reflection. Each reader may find that certain passages resonate more strongly depending on the circumstances of their life. Over time, the same psalm may reveal new layers of meaning as experiences change. The book does not exhaust itself on a single reading. It rewards return.

This continuing dialogue between reader and text is part of what gives the Psalms their enduring power. They function not simply as historical writings but as living reflections that remain open to interpretation and discovery. Each generation brings its own context to the encounter, and the Psalms meet that context with a flexibility that most ancient texts do not possess.

A Book That Endures

The lasting influence of the Psalms can be seen in the way they have been woven into the spiritual practices of countless communities throughout history. Their words have been sung in places of worship, whispered in moments of grief, and recited in times of celebration. They have accompanied individuals through some of the most significant moments of their lives — at bedsides, in places of exile, in moments of unexpected joy, and in the long quiet stretches of ordinary life that make up most of human experience.

This enduring presence demonstrates that the Psalms speak to something fundamental about human experience. They acknowledge the reality of hardship while continuing to point toward hope. They recognize the complexity of life while inviting readers to trust that meaning can still be found within it — not despite the difficulty, but often through it.

For modern readers, the Psalms offer a reminder that faith does not require the elimination of life's challenges. Instead, it invites individuals to engage those challenges with honesty, reflection, and trust. The psalmists were not people who had resolved every question before they began to write. They were people in the middle of their lives, carrying what they carried, and choosing to bring it before God. That choice — repeated across hundreds of poems, across centuries, across cultures — is what the book ultimately preserves and commends.

By returning to these ancient poems, readers join a long tradition of people who have sought understanding through their words. The conversation that began centuries ago continues today, inviting each generation to explore the enduring wisdom found within the Psalms.

Closing Reflection

"Praise the Lord. Praise God in his sanctuary; praise him in his mighty heavens. Praise him for his acts of power; praise him for his surpassing greatness. Let everything that has breath praise the Lord. Praise the Lord."
— *Psalm 150:1–2, 6*

The book of Psalms stands as one of the most enduring collections of spiritual reflection in human history. Across centuries and cultures, these poems have been read, sung, and recited by individuals and communities seeking language for their deepest experiences. From ancient temples to modern places of worship, from private moments of prayer to gatherings of entire congregations, the Psalms have remained a constant presence within the spiritual life of countless people.

What gives the Psalms their lasting influence is not merely their poetic beauty or historical significance. Their enduring power lies in the way they capture the realities of human experience with remarkable honesty. Within this collection, readers encounter expressions of joy and sorrow, confidence and doubt, gratitude and longing. These poems reveal individuals who were willing to speak openly about their lives while seeking understanding in their relationship with God.

The writers of the Psalms do not attempt to present faith as a simple or predictable journey. Instead, they acknowledge the complexities of life and bring those complexities into their prayers and reflections. Their words demonstrate that spiritual life unfolds within the ordinary circumstances of human existence, shaped by moments of celebration as well as seasons of uncertainty.

For modern readers, this openness offers an important invitation. The Psalms encourage individuals to approach faith with the same honesty demonstrated by the writers. Rather than hiding doubt or suppressing difficult emotions, the book shows that these experiences can become part of a meaningful conversation with God.

In this way, the Psalms challenge the assumption that faith requires perfect certainty or constant emotional stability. The writers themselves frequently wrestle with questions that remain unresolved. They ask why injustice sometimes appears to prevail. They wonder how long suffering will continue. They express longing for guidance during moments when the future feels unclear.

Yet even while raising these questions, the psalmists continue to direct their reflections toward God. Their willingness to remain engaged in this conversation reveals a deeper understanding of faith — one that includes both trust and inquiry. Faith is not portrayed as the absence of questions but as the willingness to continue seeking understanding in the midst of them.

This perspective allows the Psalms to remain meaningful for readers across generations. Although the cultural world of ancient Israel differs greatly from modern society, the inner experiences described within the book remain familiar. People today continue to encounter moments of joy, grief, uncertainty, gratitude, and hope. These experiences shape the emotional and spiritual lives of individuals just as they did thousands of years ago. The Psalms speak to these realities because they arise from the same human conditions that continue to shape life in every era. When readers encounter the words of the psalmists, they often recognize emotions and questions that mirror their own. This recognition creates a sense of connection across time, reminding readers that their experiences are part of a much larger human story.

What this book has attempted to do is clear that path. Understanding where the Psalms came from — the historical world that shaped them, the structure that organizes them, the literary form through which they communicate — removes barriers that can otherwise keep modern readers at a distance from the text. When the Psalms are approached only as a collection of familiar verses, their depth remains largely hidden. When they are understood as a carefully shaped anthology that developed across centuries, preserved through communal use, and organized with deliberate purpose, they begin to reveal dimensions that isolated reading cannot reach.

Each of the themes examined in this book — the diversity of psalm types, the five-book structure, the recurring concerns with justice and memory and praise and lament — points toward the same underlying reality: the Psalms were never meant to be encountered passively. They were written to draw readers in, to give voice to experiences that might otherwise go unspoken, and to place those experiences within a framework of ongoing relationship with God. That is what they have done for generation after generation, and it is what they continue to do.

The Psalms also model something that modern readers often find difficult: the willingness to remain with unanswered questions rather than forcing premature resolution. The psalmists do not always arrive at clarity. Some poems end mid-tension, with the circumstances still unresolved and the questions still open. This is not a failure of the writing. It is an honest reflection of how faith actually operates across much of life — not as a series of problems solved, but as a sustained orientation toward God in the midst of a world that does not always yield easy answers. The act of continuing to speak, to return, to bring each new season before God — that itself is what the Psalms depict as faithfulness. Not certainty arrived at, but conversation maintained.

That sustained orientation is perhaps what the Psalms commend most consistently. Not a particular emotional state. Not a specific theological conclusion. But a posture — one that keeps turning toward God through joy and grief alike, through certainty and confusion, through praise that comes easily and lament that does not resolve. The writers of the Psalms maintained that posture across very different circumstances, and the collection they left behind is evidence of how much such a posture can hold.

For readers who now return to the Psalms with this broader understanding in place, the book is likely to feel different than it did before. Passages that once seemed like isolated encouragements may now appear as part of a longer conversation. Psalms that once felt unfamiliar or uncomfortable may now be recognizable as honest voices from within the tradition — voices that have something to say precisely because they did not pretend that faith was simpler than it is.

The invitation the Psalms extend has not changed across the centuries. It is the same invitation it has always been: to bring what is real, to speak honestly, to remember what has come before, and to remain in the conversation — even when, perhaps especially when, the answers have not yet arrived.

That conversation began long before any of us. It will continue long after. The Psalms endure because the questions they carry are not going away, and because the posture of honest, persistent faith they model is one that every generation has found it necessary to learn again.

The Bible for Modern Life Series

This book is part of **The Bible for Modern Life** series—an ongoing collection that explores the meaning, historical setting, and message of individual books of Scripture.

Each volume looks closely at the biblical text to help readers understand what it meant in its original context and how its truths still apply to life today.

The goal is simple: to help modern readers engage more deeply with the Bible—one book at a time.

— Samuel Whitaker